How You Can Increase Your Sales In Any Economy

Leading Authorities Share Tips, Tools, and Secrets to Help You Dramatically Increase Your Sales!

Compiled by Doug Smart

HOW YOU CAN INCREASE YOUR SALES IN ANY ECONOMY

Managing Editor: Gayle Smart
Editor: Sara Kahan
Proofing Editor: Laura Johnson
Book Designer: Paula Chance
Copyright ©2002

All rights reserved. No portion of this book may be reproduced in any form without written permission from the publisher.

Disclaimer: This book is a compilation of ideas from numerous experts who have each contributed a chapter. As such, the views expressed in each chapter are those of the authors and not necessarily the views of James & Brookfield Publishers.

For more information, contact:
James & Brookfield Publishers
P.O. Box 768024
Roswell, GA 30076
℅ 770-587-9784

Library of Congress Catalog Number 2002113492

ISBN: 0-9712851-4-4

10 9 8 7 6 5 4 3 2 1

Contents

The Silent Sell
    Patti Wood, M.A., CSP .... *Page 05*

Stop Selling and Telling —
    Start Partnering and Positioning
    Edie Raether, M.S., CSP .... *Page 21*

Write Your Career!
    Larry Sheldon .... *Page 33*

Sell More Products and Services
Through the Power of Networking
    Debra J. Schmidt, M.S. .... *Page 47*

Your Price is Too High
    Al Tetrault, M.B.A. .... *Page 59*

Room 4$
    Mary E. Cremeans, M.B.A. .... *Page 71*

Understanding Your Customer
    Sara Owens .... *Page 89*

Convictable Commitment
    The Key to Achieving Your Goals
    Andre L. Beaudoin .... *Page 103*

The Winning Mindset in Sales
    Dr. Bill Newman .... *Page 119*

Selling Tools
    D.J. Harrington, CSP .... *Page 135*

Resource Listing .... *Page 147*

THE SILENT SELL

by Patti Wood, M.A., CSP

"The great phase of man's advancement is that in which he passes from subconscious to conscious control of his own mind and body."

F.M. Alexander,
Man's Supreme Inheritance

Imagine you are going on a sales call or to meet with a customer. Ten to ninety seconds after you walk into the room, before you're even comfortable in your chair, you may have won or lost the sale. You may spend an hour answering questions and explaining your company or product or job qualifications, but studies indicate that purchasers form a strong bias for or against you within seconds of greeting you.

What are they observing in those critical seconds? Your nonverbal communication. When we meet a stranger, we're unsure how to interact with him — we don't know his temperament or opinions — basically, we don't know if he bites! So we very quickly assess him, place him in a category, and respond accordingly. While you may study and work and plan what you will say to your customer, your nonverbal communication — the silent sell — may deliver a message you had not intended to send.

You can send up to 10,000 nonverbal cues in less than one minute of interaction with a customer. Your customer is using those cues to assess you and make decisions about whether or not to do business with you. According to current sales research, 70 percent of the prospect's impressions of you come from your body language and image, 20 percent from your voice, and 10 percent from what you say. While you cannot control all your nonverbal cues, it is important to be aware of them and do what you can to create powerful body language.

After forming a first impression of you, a prospect tends to gather information that confirms the decision already made. Although he can change his mind, it makes your job harder if that initial impression is negative. If a customer looks up from her desk as you stand in the doorway, tells you to come in, and then looks down and continues to process paperwork without even raising her eyes as you walk into her office, much less stand to shake hands, she has sent you a message about her first impression of you.

You know about those first impressions. If your gut tells you that the prospect is interested in detail, then you respond to questions in a detailed manner. If it says this person is warm and personal, then you give long responses.

In the silent sell you need to monitor how YOU are coming across to the customer. Notice whether the prospect makes eye contact with you and whether she orients the front of her body toward you. If not, ask yourself, "Did I just say something about my product or service she didn't like? Did I just say something to turn her off?"

In this situation, you have the opportunity to recover by

changing your nonverbal message or bringing it up to the verbal level. You can say something such as, "What else would you like to know about our service contract?" Or, "What else can I tell you that will help you make this decision?"

The most important thing to remember in any interaction is to let your body language reflect who you are because you want someone to buy from you or hire you. If customers are going to buy your product or service, they need to believe in and trust you. Many times people seek information about body language because they fear being themselves and feel the need to put on an act or disguise their real nature. But this chapter isn't meant to give guidance on how to be an actor. Rather, this is guidance on how to be more confident about yourself and more confident with others — and how to let others know it. Using effective body language simply means you reduce negative cues and increase positive ones. Here are ten body language tips for using effective body language in sales:

1. Think and Wait "Up"

When I go in to meet clients, I will often stand. I feel stronger and more powerful if I am already standing "up" when someone comes to greet me. You actually have more energy standing than you do when you sit. The balance of having both your feet on the ground gives you more power and strength.

Sometimes the person with whom you have an appointment will be the one who greets you. If you are nervous, you are better off standing than sitting. That way, you can walk around. If you must sit, sit at the edge of the chair with your feet firmly on the ground, so that when the person comes out to get you, you can rise up very quickly out of the chair instead of being sunk down into it. Place your briefcase by your left side so that you can pick it up with your left hand and shake with your right. Even better, get up, shake hands, and then pick up your case.

If you are giving a sales presentation at a meeting where you might normally sit, try standing. The research says you will look more like an authority on your topic and you will be given more attention and respect. To make this upright position more comfortable, give yourself an excuse to stand up. Put posters or a flip chart on the wall and use it to chart numbers or gather responses, or stand to give the heavy data portion of the presentation that might otherwise be ignored in a sit-down presentation.

2. Match Them in the First Few Minutes

Match the friendliness or the formality of the greeting you receive. Match the energy level. Pay attention to the pace and match it. Most people are uncomfortable with strangers. We like people who are like us and we are more comfortable with someone who is similar to us. By matching, you are showing the prospect that you are like them. And the research shows we are more likely to purchase from someone like us.

If a prospect answers the phone and says "hello" in a soft, low voice and you respond with a loud energetic voice, you will sound strange and different. People will shut down or shorten the interaction to get rid of that which makes them uncomfortable — you. If you are on the phone or face to face with your prospect, match and mirror that person in the critical first few minutes. If the customer talks slowly with a lot of long, silent pauses, don't interrupt or jump in with your fast-paced, rapid-fire repartee. Match the customer's relaxed communication style. Here is the formula:

1. Start with your own comfortable, confident body language.

2. Stay present with the customer; observe nonverbal cues.

3. Consciously match those cues to establish rapport.

4. If the customer is uncomfortable or shows any closed off cues, slowly and subtly move in to match those cues, then notice the internal click when you "get" how the other person is feeling. Slowly move out into a more open and relaxed posture. Once you have matched them and shown empathy, the customer will subconsciously feel more comfortable and be ready to match your more positive posture.

A small, subtle way to see if you have rapport with a prospect is to nod your head as you say something positive about the product or service. If the prospect nods too, he or she is with you! This technique is also a way to create agreement on an issue or price, as we release positive chemicals in our brains when we nod our head and we think, "Yes."

3. Get a Grip

Practice your handshake!

1. Smile and stretch out your arm towards the other person

as you approach, indicating that you want to shake hands. An arm that is held too closely to the side of the body indicates timidity and a lack of confidence.

2. Offer an equal handshake, full open palm towards the other person with your thumb on top, rather than palm down which makes you dominate.

3. Place your palm against the other person's palm so that the palms have full contact. Do not arch your palm; lay it flat. Lock thumbs and squeeze firmly but briefly.

4. Pump up and down an average of 3-5 times, the fewer the pumps the less formal the greeting. (Match the number of pumps to the corporate culture.)

5. Don't feel the need to crush the other person's hand or to shake with both of your hands. The rule is to match the pressure or gauge it not more than two additional steps in pressure. Don't have a shaking contest.

Tips:

If you have a problem with clammy hands, don't forget to wipe them on your handkerchief or tissue before you shake hands. And, at social functions, hold any iced drinks in your left hand, so your right hand will not be cold and damp when you need to shake hands.

If you are a man and you are wondering what to do in terms of shaking hands with a woman, simply match the firmness of her grip. Do not grab her hand too lightly. Business women don't mind a firm handshake. In business interactions women prefer to have their grip matched. They do not like wimpy handshakes any more than men do.

You want palm-to-palm contact in the grip as well. The opposite of a good, strong palm contact is the weak handshake when you just get fingers. My research on handshakes and greetings shows that having palm to palm contact is the most important part of the handshake. The palms of the hands are read subconsciously for messages of honesty and self-disclosure. Full contact indicates subliminally, "I am willing to be honest and self-disclosing." It is not the lack of a strong grip but the lack of palm to palm contact in a wimpy handshake that will cause someone to think, "What is he hiding? What is he keeping from me?"

4. Get Comfortable, Be Open

A general rule is to be comfortable. If you're standing, be relaxed. If you're in a chair, don't fold up and get tense.

When you are in a sales situation, you may feel nervous, especially when your prospects fire those difficult questions or objections. During these times, stay open. Don't close down your body, don't cross your legs, don't take up very little space, don't cross your arms. As soon as you do these things, your body becomes more tense, and you begin to feel emotionally tense as well. Body language is highly symbolic. If a rabbit and lion are coming down a jungle path, which one gets tense and small? The rabbit. You want powerful-lion body language. Just don't eat your prospect. Your posture and demeanor affect your image and the quality of your interaction. So don't cross your arms. Relax slightly and take up some space. If it is comfortable, try to keep your legs uncrossed.

It's okay to cross your legs at other times during a sales call, but if you are asked a complex question, uncross them. It is easier for us to process information with both feet planted firmly on the ground. That's another reason I tell people to stand in the waiting room — because you can think faster.

The most important general recommendation is to keep your body from getting tense. Hold your body in a relaxed and confident manner, and you will begin to feel that way emotionally. This position may involve sitting on the edge of the chair or sitting way back. It depends on the nature of the interaction.

What you don't want to do is to be more relaxed or more tense than the person you are with. Remember the importance of matching in the first few minutes. Stay unfolded. A folded position closes you down from revealing information and taking in information. In our culture, people tend to interpret that posture as defensive.

5. Smiling Eyes

When we tell a customer to "have a nice day" with no eye contact and a smile as flat and closed as a sealed envelope, we are sending a nonverbal message that is different from our words. When the message we send nonverbally is different from our verbal message, the customer is going to ignore the words and believe the silent sell. An insincere message does not make a customer believe you.

Generally, it is helpful to smile. Every sales book tells you that, but you may not know why. There are actually several reasons: one, you create positive chemicals in your brain when you smile; two, smiling is a "harmless" cue that makes you look less threatening and more friendly (looking friendly and harmless is especially important in cold calls and over-the-counter sales); three, the customer is likely to mirror your smile and feel good too and associate that positive feeling with purchasing from you.

A caveat! Women have to be careful. When women share serious information in a sales presentation, such as their statistics about growth of the market, the safety features of a product, or the price, they shouldn't smile. Otherwise, the information is not viewed as credible and is not taken as seriously as it is when communicated by a man. Men expect women to smile; most women have heard, on their non-smiling days, "Why aren't you smiling?"

Maintain as much eye contact as possible. Eye contact is a basic cue of friendliness. A window to your thoughts. We need to look at the eyes to tell what a person is going to do next. A lack of contact from you makes others wonder what you are keeping from them. Don't worry if you find yourself looking off to find the answer to a question. That is quite natural and everyone expects it. But after you have thought of your response and are relating it, make some eye contact.

6. Work Close

Space and territory are critical in sales situations. You will have no difficulty finding where the limits of a prospect's personal space lie. The moment you approach, the prospect will exhibit one of the "you-are-trespassing" signals: hunching, rocking, turning or looking away, drumming fingers, masking, and, most frequently, moving or leaning away to reestablish distance.

There are several advantages to working *close*:

1. Typically we sit and stand near to people we are close to on an emotional, personal level. When you get near, the prospect rearranges his or her impersonal, unemotional relationship with you to accommodate the change in physical proximity.

2. You're better able to see and read the prospect's signals.

3. The other person is better able to read all the strong, confident, and believable signals you are sending.

4. Distance suggests fear. Go in as close as is appropriate

5. Your proximity forces prospects to pay closer attention; they pick up on more of your crucial sales points.

7. Hands Down

Don't put your hand to your mouth. If you are unsure of your response or if you are not very confident about it, you want to make this motion with your hand. Don't do it! It is perceived as being deceptive. Be careful of moistening or licking your lips after an important statement. Although we sometimes do this when we are nervous before we say something, if done after we say something, it is often viewed subliminally as a sign that what we are saying is a lie. Our lips and tongue are erasing the lie.

Gestures are fine, but avoid repeating the same gesture over and over. Few gestures, done once, are bothersome, but repetitive gestures can be annoying. Try to keep your palms open. Open palms symbolize you are open and willing to self-disclose. Make sure to avoid showing the backs of your hands, slicing the air with your hands, jabbing, or pointing. These signals are read as symbolic weapons, and the prospect may think you are shooting him, stabbing him, or cutting him to pieces, all of which might make him a little uncomfortable.

8. Leaning for Meaning

When you feel emphatic about something and you want to indicate that you are charged about it, lean forward. When you want to show that you're knowledgeable and confident, say something important and then lean back in your chair. These movements will show you are confident with your expertise. When you tell someone the price or ask for the sale, be neither too far forward or back. Take your middle position, then freeze. If you lean forward after you make a request, you may seem too aggressive. If you lean back, you signal a retreat, and the prospect will debate the price or turn down the sale.

We all tend to tilt our heads to the side as we listen to people. It is not necessarily a bad habit. However, women have to be especially careful because this posture can be seen as subservient or a sign of uncertainty. If you do it too much, it will detract from your power. In some animal groups, subordinates tilt their heads to bare their neck to the dominant male of the pack. The symbolism is significant. A head straight on and straight up is powerful, but a head tilted to the side is not nearly as strong.

9. Sounds of Silence

Do not be afraid of silence. Some interviewers and executives deliberately create silence to see what you will do with it. Silence is a profound nonverbal communicator, and some people try to see how comfortable you can be with it and how you respond to it. There are two instances when comfort with silence is critical. The first is when you ask what questions a customer has (Note, the wording "What questions do you have about…?" is more open than "any questions?") Though many people will have questions ready, certain people will need eight to fifteen seconds to think of a question, analyze whether it's a good question, think about how it may be received, word it, and practice the delivery in their heads. This particular type of a communicator is likely to be more technically oriented. Engineers, scientists, or computer technicians are famous for leaving that long awkward silence after a question. Be comfortable with it. You can say "Let me give you a few moments to think about what else you would like to know about the product . . ." Or if there is a group, you can ask them to turn to someone next to them and collaborate to come up with a question.

Silence is also important when you ask for the sale. Imagine you have asked for the sale, the contract is out, you have a pen ready . . . then silence. Resist the urge to fill up the awkward pause with words. Let the other person feel awkward. The only way the feeling will stop is if they say something!

If the silence occurs at other times and is truly uncomfortable, rehearse comments you might want to offer or questions you might want to ask.

10. Get Up and Go

When you leave, stand up straight and tall, shake hands, and then pick up your things. Make sure the handshake is strong. Practice what you are going to say and have your closing well rehearsed. Keep orienting your body toward the prospect as you are exiting. As you get to the exit, turn and say, "Thank you." Make significant eye contact as you are saying your thanks, and then turn and go. Don't feel that you have to back out of the office.

The key to the silent side of communicating is to stay calm and relaxed throughout the process. You can always speak up if you feel you've lost the sale. Bring it up to the verbal level and say something about it. Now that you have learned the steps to the silent sell, take this self-evaluation tool to assess what you are doing to create powerful body language.

Ask yourself:
What are my three best qualities?

1. _____

_____

2. _____

_____

3. _____

_____

How do I express these qualities nonverbally when I am selling?

_____

_____

_____

_____

What am I doing and what can I do to create powerful body language in the silent sell?

_____

_____

_____

_____

About
Patti Wood, M.A., CSP

Patti Wood, M.A., CSP is an international speaker and trainer. Since 1982 she has designed and conducted keynote speeches, workshops and convention seminars for hundreds of top companies and national associations. Clients include: AT&T, GTE, Chick-fil-A, Dupont, Elli Lilly, Merck Pharmaceuticals, Lucent Technologies, The Kroger Company, Nortel Networks, Price Waterhouse, Nextel, Hewlett Packard, and hundreds more. Clients describe her as a dynamic, high-energy, powerhouse presenter. Patti develops high-energy information-packed programs and laughter-filled relationships with participants that leave them talking in the halls about what they've learned. Patti has been researching, writing and speaking on nonverbal communication for more than 20 years, and has taught communication at the university level for 11 years. She is interviewed frequently by the media, including CBS and ABC radio news, the BBC, PBS, The Discovery Channel, Entrepreneur Magazine, Woman's World, The Washington Post, Cosmopolitan, The National Examiner, YM J-14, First for Women, and Expert Magazine as a body language expert. Time Magazine recognized her nonverbal communication course at Florida State University as one of the top college courses in the country. She is a communication consultant for US Weekly and has written seven books and co-authored four. Her research on nonverbal communication led to her position as the National Spokesperson for Wrigley's Spearmint gum.

Contact Information:
Patti Wood
2312 Hunting Valley Drive
Decatur, GA 30033
Phone: (404) 371-8228
E-mail: Pattiwood@PattiWood.com
Website: www.PattiWood.com
www.TheBodyLanguageLady.com

Stop Selling and Telling— Start Partnering and Positioning

by Edie Raether, MS, CSP

Selling in tough times may be easier than you think! It is a matter of what you are selling, to whom you are selling, and how you are selling. The game may have changed, but have you? Since we tend to be creatures of habit, we often become victims of the *Insanity Principle*, which is doing the same thing over and over and expecting different results. The problem with repetition may be that you are using sales techniques and a selling style that once rewarded you well but may no longer be effective. It is smart to keep up with the times. The good news is, when the economic climate changes, *new opportunities emerge*. Until recently, more millionaires were made during America's Great Depression than any other time period. Our ability to see and seize those opportunities determines our success in an ever-changing marketplace.

Andy Kessler said, "Fire your sales force and empower your customer." As corporations access and communicate directly with their customers and create direct sales channels through internal networks and clients, the cost per sale will be lower than through existing sales channels. Salespeople will remain valuable assets in the selling equation, but their role has changed to information agent, problem solver, and facilitator. This does not mean the human element will be displaced by technology. In fact, long-term relationships with salespeople who understand their situation will become more important. Knowledge is power. Thus, those with the most information will have the most power. As a sales agent, your role will be more that of a synthesizer of information provided by the customer. Thereafter you will implement necessary changes, establishing a process of information to transformation. The ultimate change agent is technology. If you do not use the tools technology provides to build your business, others will build theirs at your expense. To be effective, you must be efficient. With a current emphasis on relationship-based selling, rather than the transaction-based selling of the past, and as customers seek solutions rather than products, we must alter our mode of operation. The fact is that solutions don't work if people don't want them.

Although some people maintain a conservative, practical purchasing style, it is actually in economic down-times that consumers experience psychological deprivation and thus indulge themselves in luxuries or non-essential purchases. For example, the sales of Harley-Davidson motorcycles continue to soar as dealers maintain a wait-list for those eager to share in the identity of owning a "hog." The average Steinway grand piano sells for over $50,000.00 and yet sales continue to rise in the recession of the new century. Victoria's Secret and Bodyworks also sell those non-essentials which seem to become essential when people feel deprived or fear being without. Certainly since September 11, people have become more indulgent in life's simple pleasures and refuse to postpone sensory indulgence, preferring instead to live in the "now." Then too, with the stock market plunging and the Enron and WorldCom accounting scandals, people have lost confidence in investments which promised a bright financial future and guaranteed personal security. These significant events along with the technology revolution have altered the values and thus the buying habits of consumers. Your challenge is not only to understand the effects of socio-economic factors, but to also understand how the customer's mind works, for it ultimately dictates all buying behaviors. You must get at the heart of the matter by developing your emotional and intuitive intelligence. The fact is, at least 75 percent of all decisions are based on emotion, the subconscious, or association. In other words, we decide by emotion and then justify with logic in defense of the decisions we have made. Anticipation of desperation elicits opposite responses from different people, just as general stress and pressure will cause some people to be stimulated and excel while others roll over and play dead. Some people not only survive, but actually thrive on the stimulation others perceive as a threat to their survival and react by becoming semi-comatose with anxiety.

Once you understand the economic climate and the effects it has on various people and industries, you must then assess your style of selling. Are you caught in a rut doing what you have always done or are you incorporating technology's competitive edge? Are you expanding your vision to encompass a global economy or are you continuing to sell only to the guy next door? How are you redefining your customer base to not only expand your horizons geographically, creating a wider base of possible return, but also to intensify the depth and penetration of your efforts? How are you leveraging your time? What market provides the best potential for growth, and where are you wasting time, energy, and money simply out of habit or past routines? What tasks are you doing that are not unique to your special talents and thus need to be delegated? Are there other ways that you can free up time and energy to pursue new territories, create new strategies, and implement the desired changes for competitive partnering and positioning? If you have said no to any of the above, you need to establish a system of accountability, a process which may require the assistance of a personal or business coach. You must commit yourself to all the above steps as your personal program to success. Then ask yourself these questions: "How do I create an alignment with my customers? What structures are in place to sustain customer loyalty?" For example, Jordan Kitt's Music, one of the largest Steinway piano retailers, headquartered in College Park, Maryland, offers a warranty of value. In addition to an iron-clad guarantee of best price, Kitt's also allows all instruments to be traded in for full purchase price on an upgrade to any Steinway piano for a period of fifteen years after the original purchase. What innovative ways have you created to assure a future sale and never lose a current customer to the competition?

Innovate or evaporate! Today more than ever, innovation and creativity are crucial to your professional and business survival. It is about "being" different to make a difference. In our information-saturated world, do you stand out? What is your YOUnique selling proposition? Quit playing "follow the follower" marketing, disguised as "follow the leader." Former Supreme Court Justice Felix Frankfurter said, "Anybody who is any good is different from anybody else." Not taking the risk to be different may be the one you can least afford. Having been a talk show host with ABC radio and TV, I am a loyal listener of Paul Harvey and Earl Nightingale, who exemplify the rewards of being different. When Earl Nightingale left Phoenix in 1949 with a one-way ticket to Chicago to seek employment with network radio, he was assured of failure by his colleagues who did not have the courage to step outside their comfort zones. And now you know the rest of the story! For a moment, just reflect on how you might dare to be different. The hockey star Wayne Gretzky said, "You miss 100 percent of the shots you never take."

There's no glory in being a best-kept secret. How are you "the only" in your chosen field? How do you think, talk, act, look and sell differently? Are your guarantees different? What do you offer that is different? Do you capture a different marketplace and anticipate future markets to target as the "first" one there which always supersedes being better or best. You know who was the first to land on the moon, but do you know the name of the second or third ? The fact is, hardly anyone knows or cares. While Lindbergh will always be remembered as the first solo flight across the Atlantic Ocean, very few remember the brave souls who followed his path. It's the impact of being "the first." As Al Ries and Jack Trout state in their enlightening book, *Positioning: The Battle for Your Mind,* "Positioning is not what you do to a product. Positioning is what you do to the mind of the prospect." Quit chasing customers and start attracting them by positioning yourself so they seek you and your services. People love to buy but hate to be sold. How are you positioning yourself as "the expert" in your industry? Whether it's having a column in the newspaper, being published, or being a frequent guest on targeted talk shows, you must focus your time and energies on positive positioning.

Become a magnet! Become a "sales magnet." Begin with changing your mindset or what I refer to as *MindShif*™. It is creating a routine of mind-empowering strategies which enhance performance and results. It is getting a return on investment from your intellectual capital by rebooting the brain and reprogramming the mind. In other words, you must rewire your brainware by igniting your *intuitive intelligence*™ (the other IQ) to access the power of the subconscious mind. The subconscious mind can process thousands of bits of information in just a second while the conscious mind can process only a few. The acceleration, or as Robert Copper calls it, the "exceleration" of mind processes, is crucial to make a difference in today's competitive marketplace where change has changed. In fact, even the velocity of change has changed! Time is more than money. It's often what makes it or breaks it. No great things come to those who wait, but only to those who hustle. Lee Iacocca is known for shooting from the hip, and Harry Quadrache of Square D for his famous advice, "fire, aim, ready." Both of these successful men are emphasizing the need to act intuitively and instinctually in decision-making and problem-solving. We rarely have the time to do a spread sheet and evaluate the pros and cons as in traditional, logical, linear thinking. In April of 2001, a pilot who was threatened by a Chinese bomber was applauded for his ability to so spontaneously determine how and where to land his plane safely.

Analysis paralysis is a disease no one can tolerate and no company can afford. How many more people would have perished in the disaster of September 11 had people, including the rescuers, not used gut instinct and intuitive intelligence to act swiftly?

Selling smarter, not harder, is contingent upon not only *what* we think, but *how* we think as well. Both our thoughts and our thinking style determine our chosen actions and results. Aristotle said, "We are what we repeatedly do. Excellence is not an act, it is a habit." Somewhat paradoxically, we first make our habits and then our habits make us. Og Mandino, in his classic book, *The Greatest Salesman in the World,* states, "as children we are slaves to our impulses, but as adults we become slaves to our habits, which surpass the power of free will and imprison our future."

To build habits that serve you well, I suggest that you daily commit to two important affirmations and include them in your sales strategy. *I will enjoy life with laughter and I will nourish my spiritual side.*

Men and women are the only creatures that have the gift of laughter. Laughter is the child of surprise and surprise always keeps you in awe of the world around you. When we laugh we release endorphins which increase confidence and create a state of euphoria and total well-being. It actually changes our perception and perspective of conflicts, reducing the magnitude and sense of defeat when we have lost potential sales or we fall short of our quarterly goals or projected growth. Humor helps us detach from our pain and challenging situations, allowing us emotional leverage and a chance to "get a grip" on the problem. It is only with such emotional distance that we can resolve issues and bring forth the desired change. Dr. Patch Adams is living proof that laughter pays! Perhaps you saw the movie, *Patch Adams*. In the early eighties, long before he became a celebrity, I was a speaker at a wellness conference at which Patch Adams also had spoken. I learned Patch has always been rich in his gifts, talents, and generous heart. I remember I had complained to him about feeling "used." His refreshing response was, "Well, Edie, I want to be used. In fact, my wish is to be all used up before I die." Truly, laughter changes our perspective, our attitude, and our approach to living life in a meaningful way. Norman Cousins in his book, *The Anatomy of an Illness,* shares how he used humor to heal himself and extend his enjoyment of life. If humor can change your perspective and vision, and even help heal, how might you use the power of laughter to rejuvenate yourself, to resolve differences with difficult clients, and to create the power of rapport for lasting business relationships and profitable partnerships? When God closes a door, He opens a window; however, you must crawl through. A well-respected speaker, Rosita Perez, once commented on my speaking style and message in saying, "Edie, you give people medicine, but it goes down like candy." I realized it was the humor that made the potentially hard-to-swallow message taste like candy. Losing a potential sale may hit you harder during tough times, but humor will not only help recharge your battery, it will also convert linear thinking to the more creative, lateral, out-of-the-box thinking. The "aha" springs from the "ha-ha," or, in other words, laughter ignites inspiration and triggers your creativity, which is crucial to not just surviving, but thriving in today's competitive marketplace. Laughter helps us let go of past failure and pain, rejuvenating the spirit with hope and positive expectation which, when magnified, creates a magnetic field that attracts those elements, people, and sales to manifest our desired outcomes and success.

Nourish your spiritual side. The guidance we seek is to discover who we are through a greater awareness of our purpose and mission in life. James Hillman in his incredible book, *The Soul's Code*, explains how each of us is challenged with discovering, creating and manifesting a unique purpose in life. We are not here by chance and may need to seek help and guidance to manifest our destiny. Our crises are often opportunities to learn, discover, and redirect ourselves when having lost our way or feeling too tired to continue on our life's journey. If you have any sense of mystery about the world around you, your task is to discover the path that your heart speaks. However, you must take the time to listen, for it gets louder as you come closer to unveiling the truth that gives you wings. You can only work smarter, not harder, in your chosen profession when your life's work also chooses you. You must not only have personal alignment with your clients and customers, but also with yourself. Sarah Hughes skates like a swan, and Michael Jordan shoots the basketball as if the net were magnetic, and Yo Yo Ma turns the strings of the cello into vocal cords. The fact is, those who work smarter often also work harder, they just happen to call it fun and enjoy the process. I have often confessed that I don't go to work, I go to play. Yes, you must leverage your time with the tools of technology and respond to the changing values, wants, and needs of your people with positive positioning and networking. However, when selling and sales, and partnering and positioning are fun because they reflect your special gifts and talents, all of the above suggestions will take root, allowing you to grow and prosper, but only after you plant and nurture the right seeds. Follow your intuition or inner voice and have faith in it, even if the guidance you receive is not what you had expected. Selling in any economy has more to do with you, not them or the economic climate. The answer lies within. Change comes from the "insight" out. Truth is given to different people in different ways. Accept who you are and cultivate your special gifts. You must give voice to the music of your spirit. This can all be summarized with the Hebrew word, *L' Chiam*, which means "To life!" It is not to a happy life, it is just to life. It is not like prayer, for we pray for things we don't have. We already have life. *L' Chiam.*

About
Edie Raether, M.S., CSP

A change strategist and human asset manager for over 30 years, Edie is a nationally-recognized authority on people and performance. Her mind-empowering strategies provide the power tools for mastering change from the "insight" out, transforming untapped potential into peak performance. With primary expertise in practical intuition, instinctual and emotional intelligence and thinking/behavioral styles, Edie's refreshing approach inspires action. Whether it is a seminar on leadership, team building, change, customer service, negotiations, sales, marketing or safety and stress management, Edie's motivational systems will fire 'em up! A restructuring-recovery specialist, her "thrivership" programs empower the working wounded to restore morale after crisis or layoff. More than 2500 professional associations and Fortune 50 companies have been empowered by Edie's keynotes, seminars, and follow-up coaching for sustained peak performance. Her clients include IBM, S.C. Johnson, J.C. Penney, Oscar Mayer, Marriott, General Motors, and Meeting Planners International. Edie has shared the platform with other celebrities such as Tom Brokaw, Patch Adams, Art Linkletter and Bob Hope.

Contact Information:
Edie Raether, M.S., CSP
Performance PLUS
4717 Ridge Water Court
Holly Springs, NC 27540
Phone: (919) 557-7900
Fax: (919) 557-7999
E-mail: edie@raether.com
Website: www.raether.com

WRITE YOUR CAREER!

by Larry Sheldon

The very idea that you've got to work harder to get your sales volume up or to keep your customer base happy and growing is a self-defeating concept. It speaks to the condition of your mind. With your mind in the wrong place, your focus will be, too. The smarter thing to do — not to mention the easier — is to change your mind.

In my signature keynote, *Write Your Life!*, I challenge my audience to create the life they want by simply living it like a novel. I urge them to forgo leaving it all up to fate and to write the book themselves. This approach works for almost all people in almost all aspects of their professional and personal lives. I cannot think of a place where it works better than in creating a vibrant, challenging, and fun sales career.

I struggled through far too many of my thirty years with IBM, trying to just do a little more, just push a little harder, just work a little longer in order to overcome what I perceived were the obstacles to my success. Then I realized that I was allowing others to create the scenarios in which none of my efforts seemed to garner the results warranted by the effort. Eventually, I learned that if I created the situations in which I would perform, then I could set the stage for success at the outset — and all along the way. My success quadrupled, and I was working less to achieve more.

Now that I'm a public speaker and corporate trainer, I've discovered a wonderful metaphor for making all this easy to understand and even easier to implement. If you just live your life — or your career in sales — like a novel, it will be the one you want because it's the one you create. Consider yourself an author, and *Write Your Career!*

Here are just three of the many lessons that are yours for the asking, if you will live your career like a novel. Study the explanations and examples given here, but think about how each one applies to your job, to your relationships, and to your life. Then approach the lessons one at a time, taking a couple of weeks on each, learning to make it a routine . . . a habit . . . in the new life that you are creating.

1. Take risks.

A timid author produces a timid book. It's a shaky read. Not taking risks produces a tedious textbook of a life when you ought to be writing your *magnus opus*. The same is true of your career. Think about it with temerity and it's sure to be mediocre. The author who produces a best seller isn't afraid to take risks. And we should do the same with our lives. Let me give you an example.

I remember that fairly early in my career at IBM I had become a good project manager. My job was to sell the client on a customized software development project and then to manage that project to successful conclusion. I was soon teaching others how to do the same. At one point, after several well-received classes on selling and managing the software development business, I found myself before a group of seasoned veterans from the hardware world. They weren't at all sure about this young upstart from whom they were supposed to learn something. Keeping their attention was a real challenge, and I knew it from the very moment that I began my introduction. By the time I got to the first major point in the course, half the room was on some other planet. I had to do something to gain and retain their focus. It was a time for taking risks. So, in those days of IBM blue suits and white shirts, I jumped up on one of the classroom tables and shouted, "How do you think you get the potential software customer to pay attention to you?" It worked. Everyone in the room stopped talking, jaws hanging low. I quickly added something very relevant and to the point about the topic. They were all listening now. They kept listening. I took a calculated risk, and it paid off. I've never found an opportunity that called for that technique again, but it was a risk that I'm glad I took at that moment.

The same strategies that work in your career work in all aspects of your life. As a matter of fact, learning to take risks throughout your personal, as well as your professional, life can create habits that will pay big dividends when the sales stakes are high. It's never too late ... or too soon ... to start.

For instance, when I was a very young man, I managed to get out of Texas and end up in Europe. I volunteered for the U.S. Navy, went to Officer Candidate School in Newport, Rhode Island, and then to Naval Officers' Supply School in — of all places — Athens, Georgia. Talk about "good ole boy" pork barrel politics. Can you imagine what must have transpired to ever get the Naval Officers'

Supply School located in a town hundreds of miles from the nearest ocean. But I digress. I did so well in supply school, I got my choice of the available jobs. I chose the *USS Springfield,* the Flagship of the Admiral of the 6th Fleet. It was home-ported in Villefranche-sur-mer, on the Riviera, just seven kilometers from Nice. It turned into one of the most fabulous chapters in my life's story . . . and, I'm proud to say, it's real close to the front!

Actress Grace Kelly had married Prince Rainier by then and become Princess Grace of Monaco. One of her favorite charities was the British American Hospital. She gave a benefit ball for the hospital each year on Easter weekend in the Hotel de Paris in Monte Carlo. One year, the Admiral was asked to provide a half dozen young officers as escorts for the nurses at the hospital. I volunteered right away.

Next thing I knew, I was inside the Hotel de Paris in Monte Carlo, right next door to the famous casino, surrounded by people dripping in diamonds. At one point, I saw someone dancing with Princess Grace. She was stunning. A soft breeze caressed the tinkling crystal chandeliers, causing sparkles to flash all around. The Princess was swirling around the floor in a diaphanous pink gown, strapless and billowing to the floor. In amazement, I thought: "Wow, she looks just like a movie star!" Oh, well, what can I say? I was twenty-something.

Then came the risk . . . and the payoff. I took a deep breath, walked onto the floor and, you got it, this kid in Navy dress whites cut in! I don't remember much else, except that I put my arms in the proper places and that the Princess was quite charming about it all. Moments later, one of her entourage came over, said something about urgency and whisked her out of my clutches.

It lasted only a moment, but, because of my ability to break out of my textbook tedium and take a risk, I was able to write a chapter in my book of life that has positively influenced every one of my subsequent experiences.

You can do similar things in your sales career. Don't be timid. Don't wait for others to call the shots or set the scene in motion. Volunteer to do what you want to do. And then take risks while you are doing it. Change your mind from that of tedious sales textbook to one of creative sales ingenuity. You'll be surprised at what starts happening right away.

2. Don't regress.

The second guideline to remember as a *life-author*, as the person who is creating this career, is to reread without regressing. Let me put it another way: This is not your first draft! There isn't any first draft! You don't get the privilege of editing and then living it all over. You can't go back. You can't replay the tape, build the relationship better this time, and make the sale on the second try.

Midway through my IBM career, I switched from large mainframe systems to smaller departmental systems, later called distributed processing. Success in selling these kinds of solutions over and over led to my being asked to develop a marketing course on just how to do it. The temptation was to simply stress the "make it replicable" angle, saying that once you did it successfully with one customer, you could do it that way with every other customer. I intuitively knew that was not true. We ended up developing the class around a case study that participants worked on for several days. Every so often, we would throw in some unpredictable customer reaction, so that the replicable solutions that were being proposed had to be changed, if even slightly, to make them fit the new situation. I didn't know it at the time, but I was teaching people to reread their past chapters for lessons learned, without getting trapped in them. They were rereading without regressing.

To be sure, you should use your memories . . . even your mistakes . . . as valuable lessons, but you must reread parts of your novel without regressing. Regressing means trying to live in the past. It's a sad existence. It's more like a history book than a novel. And we all know how boring they can be! If you take a close look, you'll probably discover that you do regress over and over.

I'm sorry to say that it happened to my mom. She started out writing the most fabulous novel, reminiscent of the happiest parts of an F. Scott Fitzgerald story. She grew up in Smithville, Texas, a little town about forty miles south of Austin. Mom was actually crowned "Miss Smithville" in 1932. She was drop-dead gorgeous.

My dad played in the Mack Rogers Band. Remember the Tommy Dorsey Band and the Glenn Miller Band from what we now call the "big band" era? Well, the Mack Rogers Band was a very well-known regional band, headquartered in San Antonio. They often toured Texas doing one night dances. Dad played the tuba for them . . . and he drove their tour bus. He was handsome and totally charismatic. Everybody loved him. And he loved Mom — from the very first time he laid eyes on her at that dance in Austin.

They dated. Soon they were married. And Mom began a fairy tale existence. They lived in the Gunter Hotel, the place to see and be seen, in downtown San Antonio. Mom's initial experiences at cooking involved charming the hotel's chef into preparing something not on the room service menu! Every evening, the Mack Rogers Band played for dinner and dancing at the Gunter. And every night Mom would dress in some flowing, mid-length cocktail frock. She'd often put a gardenia in her long, jet-black hair. Her ruby red lips glistened, her complexion virtually glowed, and she looked like she had just sprung forth — live — right off of the screen at the huge Majestic Theatre across the street.

Mom would float off the elevator into the dining room. As soon as Mack saw her, he'd wave his baton. Instantly, the band would stop whatever they were playing and break directly into Mom and Dad's special song. I told you: it was a fairy tale existence. It was a magnificent chapter. But — as it will — life changed. My dad had an accident in the bus. The Mack Rogers Band dissolved. Mom and Dad moved to the Rio Grande Valley, where he became the local Grand Prize beer distributor. He also promptly became an alcoholic. I was born, but within a few years they were divorced.

Mom went on to marry twice more. But she never really made a go of it. She was always talking about being "Miss Smithville" or about life at the Gunter Hotel. She regressed into that wonderful past, and she was never able to write another chapter in her book that came anywhere near it. She could have reread, learned, not regressed, and moved forward. But she didn't.

Do you see any of yourself in this story? Do you catch yourself trying to relive that glorious sale you made once with that happiest of customers? You can't expect the next situation to be like the last. It won't be exactly like any that you've ever lived through before. So don't get trapped in regression. Don't try to make them all alike. Use your mind to *reread* for the lessons to be learned, but apply them in new and creative ways to new situations.

Just remember that *writer's block* is what happens when all you can do is the same thing you've done before, in exactly the same way. And writer's block is an awful thing to let happen to your one and only autobiography. That's what this sales career you've chosen is, you know — your autobiography — or, at least, a big part of it. Live it like a novel. Make it exciting for you and for those around you. It just depends on your mindset.

3. Re-create — just keep reinventing.

This advice goes for your career and your life. Know without a doubt that you can always turn the page and start a new chapter. You hold the pen. No one else does. So you can declare one chapter over and begin a new one anytime you choose.

You may feel that you've been through some pretty difficult situations in your life in customer service and sales. You probably have. But you never know when it might get worse. Yet this is a lesson in hope.

When I was diagnosed as HIV positive, I was devastated. Back then, in the early 1990s, when they told you that you were HIV positive, they also unequivocally told you that you were going to die. What was unspoken, but what you heard, was, "And you are going to die right away!"

Through a river of tears, I rewrote my will. I created a directive to physicians. I fashioned appropriate health care and general powers of attorney. I even planned my funeral and memorial service.

But I didn't die. Oh, I got sick. I had to start taking awful, toxic, nauseating pills. But I didn't die. So I turned to God . . . to my own personal spirituality. I spent hours with myself, alone, in the quiet, listening for the voice I could not hear. And, then, finally it came. It was God talking. Or was it me talking? Just me talking to me? Does it matter?

I heard this voice say, "Larry, you've at least got a few chapters left. Are you really going to let them be boring?" Suddenly, I knew that's not what I wanted. I just couldn't. I just wouldn't. That's when I began consciously *life-writing* again.

I began getting out of the house, being with people, working in several organizations. I began living to the fullest again. Then one day, I noticed something. My main character, me, the one this book was all about, had changed. He was gentler, more vulnerable, more willing to risk hurt — and, possibly, even rejection — for the very promise of love. And, you know what? I liked him a lot better, not in spite of, but because of the very pain he had been through.

That was almost ten years ago. And, I'm still here. I'm still living. I'm still writing. I learned over a long period of mourning to simply turn the page one day and start a new chapter. And, every day, I say: "Thank you, God, for turning on a newer and brighter lamp so that I can see more clearly."

HIV has been a huge challenge for me. But I began practicing this idea of constantly recreating life early in my professional career. I never kept the same job more than a few years throughout the thirty I spent with IBM. That was, indeed, by design. Whenever I felt that I was getting stale at something, just because I had been doing it for some time, I found a way to change what I was doing

... usually with a promotion! Sometimes, it was because I wanted to live in a particular place . . . like Heidelberg, Germany or Montreal, Canada . . . both assignments that I created. At other times it was because I wanted the excitement of the challenge, like creating an executive briefing center for the highest level customer executives involved in sales decisions focusing on the advantages of IBM's tiniest semiconductor technologies . . . a seemingly impossible task! Always, it was because I knew that I could keep things exciting, keep things moving forward, keep creating the career I wanted by simply turning the page and starting a new chapter.

You can do the same. Don't let the loss of one sale or one customer seem like the end of your story. Turn the page and start a new chapter. Every past experience you've had, good or bad, is fuel to make your newer, brighter lamp help you see more clearly. With this attitude, every chapter you write will be better than the one before.

Writing Your Life and Your Career Like a Novelist

There are many more lessons than these three to be learned from the metaphor of living life like a novel. One says that as the author of your own book, your own career, you have to understand that the end of a plotline is not the end of your whole story. A lost sale, especially a big one that perhaps would span a delivery period of a year or more, is a loss indeed. But it's the end of a plotline. Your big story, the life of your career, goes on. Get busy and recreate something, reinvent something, move forward.

A similar lesson from our metaphor informs us that it's OK to write characters out of our story. Just think about the great books of literature or even the daily soap operas. When characters are no longer useful to the new direction in which the story is headed, they move away or die or just fade into the background. It really is OK to write characters, even customers, out of your sales story. Just know why you are doing it. Make it a conscious decision.

The parallels go on and on. Just like the author of a novel, we — as authors of our own destinies — must weave a fabric of interdependent subplots that make the story interesting and the characters engrossing. We must take risks. We must reread for learning's sake, but never regress. We must constantly recreate and reinvent our lives and our careers.

I can't think of a better role model to sum up these lessons than my Aunt Leo. She understands new chapters better than anybody I know. Aunt Leo is 95 years old. She still lives alone in her own house in McAllen, Texas. She doesn't drive anymore, but she swears she still could if she wanted to. She wouldn't mind taking the risk, but Aunt Leo at least has compassion for the rest of us.

Actually, Aunt Leo's name is Ladelle, but everyone in the family calls her Leo. I know — that's a man's name. I don't know why we've always called her that. It's just a Texas thing, I guess.

Anyway, five years ago, Aunt Ladelle had a quadruple bypass. They split her ribs open, ripped some veins out of her legs, and rebuilt four of the arteries around her heart. Three years ago, they stuck a tube into her knee, put her in the hospital for a week to drain fluids, and then replaced some cartilage. Two years ago, they slit the skin on her chest and installed a pacemaker. But Aunt Ladelle just keeps writing new chapters.

Last Christmas, I went to see her. Over coffee, out of the blue, she asked: "Larry, how do you like my eyebrows?" I was taken by surprise. Aunt Ladelle had always showered, dressed, and put on makeup before appearing to the household. I muttered, "Why they look fine . . . like always, Ladelle."

She explained, "You know, Larry, I was taking three hours every morning in the bathroom just getting myself ready for the day. Then I realized, over half that time was on these eyebrows. I'd put on eyebrow pencil and then have to wipe it off. One would be higher than the other. Or one would be crooked. Just wipe, draw, re-wipe, re-draw. It was taking forever, and I was getting depressed. I felt stuck in a trap. So a couple months ago, I said to my granddaughter, "Linda, you know that place you go to get your eyes done. I want to go. So we went in, and I just had them tattooed on! Now I get up in the morning . . . and there they are!"

Aunt Ladelle's body is slowly being replaced, part by part, but she's still writing her chapters. And when she gets *writer's block*, she just flat does something about it. Pretty great for 95, wouldn't you say?

Aunt Ladelle worked most of her life. Almost all of that time she was in sales. Not with some big corporation, but just in small settings. At first she was a cashier in a restaurant. Then she kept the office and the sales floor going when my uncle opened a small manufacturing plant. And, finally, she did all the selling when they opened a south Texas antique shop, and he was away all the time buying. She knew then what she still knows now: how to keep living life like a novel, especially when you're selling. Aunt Ladelle looks back on a long, adventurous life, and she is content because she feels she had the freedom that comes with creating your own life.

John Crudele, CSP, a colleague of mine in the National Speakers Association, puts it wonderfully. He says, "You think freedom is getting what you want. But the ultimate freedom comes at the end of your life, when you realize you wanted just what you got."

I don't know how you can do that at the end of your life or at the end of your sales career unless you've been writing your own story as you go along.

You're writing your career, whether you know it or not. So far, your career-novel may have been a best seller or a bust . . . but there's still time to turn it into a blockbuster.

From now on, in every thought, in every decision, in every action, in every good deed, in every adventure, in every challenge, in every incredible joy and every heart-breaking sadness, in every moment . . . just live your life like a novel.

Create your own career. The one you want. Author your own masterpiece. And just keep writing until your inkwell is totally dry.

About Larry Sheldon

*L*arry Sheldon spent nearly thirty years in the fast-paced and high energy world of International Business Machines. He was consistently recognized as a unique and highly skilled communicator. He was acknowledged as a superior manager, an inspiring leader, a gifted instructor and an innovative thinker. He presented workshops all over the U.S., as well as in London, Edinburgh (Scotland), Lisbon, Sindelfingen (Germany), Tokyo, Montreal and Toronto. He was a "main tent" speaker at large customer conferences in Atlanta, Sydney, Melbourne, Frankfurt, Mexico City and Tokyo. After retiring from IBM, Larry documented what he does to communicate and lead successfully. Based in Atlanta, he now speaks to large and small groups and teaches seminars and workshops through his private consulting practice. Areas of expertise include Interpersonal Communications & Presentation Skills, Leadership, Team Building, Board Development and Renewal, Personnel Policy, Strategic Planning, Project Management and Diversity Training.

Contact Information:
Larry Sheldon
Shelco Creative Consulting
951 Glenwood Avenue, Suite 2907
Atlanta, GA 30316-1893
Phone: (404) 624-1721
Fax: (404) 624-1721
E-mail: larrysheldon@shelco.net
Website: www.shelco.net

Sell More Products and Services
Through the Power of Networking

by Debra J. Schmidt, M.S.

Networking is an art based on a set of skills that must be mastered in order for you to make connections and build positive relationships. The more you refine your networking skills, the more you'll see your success reflected through business growth, more sales, bigger promotions, better jobs, and even a better quality of life.

Many people think networking is about meeting as many people as you can, telling them about yourself, and handing out hundreds of business cards. Networking is *not* schmoozing. If you contact people only when business is down or you're trying to sell something, you'll achieve dismal results. When you spend too much time pushing your own needs, people get your number quickly and run when they see you coming.

There are eight basic networking principles you must apply to achieve networking success. When you master these simple techniques, these principles will become powerful connection tools that will help you build your client base and grow your business. You can use most of these connection tools at every social function, professional association meeting, community event, and golf outing you attend.

Connection Tool 1: Work The Room

When you first arrive at an event, don't head straight for the group of people you know. If you surround yourself with friends and co-workers, you will create barriers between yourself and prospective clients. That doesn't mean you shouldn't be friendly and sociable with your friends, but make a point of trying to meet at least one new person at every event. Then, spend quality time talking with that person so you can begin to establish trust and rapport.

If you're at an event sponsored by your company or a professional organization, limit your time at the cocktail bar. Use caution about drinking alcohol in front of your clients or prospects. Many view it as unprofessional.

At most events, there will be a reception before the program begins. Even if your company is not hosting the event, you can use this time to make the guests feel valued. Greet people and thank them for attending.

A great question to ask others is "How did you happen to become involved with this organization?" When they answer, follow up with, "Really? Tell me more about that." The most important thing is to get the other person talking about their interests, then *listen*.

Offer to introduce people to your contacts to help them build their own networks. Also remember, to burn a bridge is to burn your future. Never say anything negative about anyone or imply agreement with another person who is criticizing someone, even if it's done with humor. Your comments may come back to bite you.

When you are networking at any event, your personal credibility is not the only thing at stake.

Your positive networking skills are a reflection on your company as well. Focus on what you can do for others. If someone tells you about his or her business, ask "What makes you unique in your field and sets you apart from others? I'd like to learn as much as I can about you and your business so I can tell others about you."

You may feel awkward trying out some of these ideas, but don't get discouraged. Networking takes practice, and every event represents a perfect opportunity to begin to solidify the skills you need to be a pro. If you are new to networking, start with low-risk environments like dinner out with friends or your children's soccer games. Who knows, you may end up with one or two solid leads as a result of trying out your new networking skills.

Connection Tool 2: Give More Than You Hope to Gain

Successful people are viewed as resources for advice, information, and contacts. Be on the lookout for ways to send business leads, job candidates, and other resources to your clients and prospective clients.

For example, one of my clients called me to ask if I knew of any college student looking for a summer job. This company runs a major tour program that gets extremely busy during the summer months, and she was in need of quality employees. I told her I'd see what I could do to help.

After we hung up, I located my list of contacts at area universities and colleges. The people I knew were the deans of journalism and mass communications departments. I immediately faxed a letter to each of them outlining the available summer positions. I emphasized the advantages of these jobs for students majoring in their departments. They would get experience in special-event planning, public speaking, networking, and more. Each dean posted the letter in his or her department and encouraged students to consider applying.

My client was flooded with qualified job applicants. When she called to thank me, she asked how I had accomplished this feat. I shared my contact list and a copy of the letter with her so she could send out her own notices. She continues to use my idea each year to recruit student candidates to fill those summer positions.

The whole project took me about two hours and did not generate any immediate business from that client. But I'm at the top of her list whenever she needs to hire a trainer or a consultant because she knows I put her business first.

Connection Tool 3: Actively Listen

Listening is one of the most powerful networking tools, but most people have very weak listening skills. You can't actively listen to a person and do anything else. So, whether you're networking on the phone or face-to-face, when someone is talking to you, stop whatever you're doing. That means you can't be looking at someone else, banging away on your laptop, taking notes, or glancing at your watch. Some people call such activities multi-tasking — others call it bad manners.

Get the other person talking about his or her interests. A question I love to ask after someone has told me what business he's in is "What's keeping you up at night?" You'd be surprised by the answers. A way to keep someone talking is to say "How interesting, tell me more about that."

Quality, not quantity, is the key to networking success. When you go to an event, focus on spending the evening with no more than one or two individuals to give yourself the opportunity to build solid relationships.

Don't flit around the room passing out your business cards or look over the shoulders of the people you're chatting with to see who your next target is. You will hurt your own credibility because people will think you're being insincere.

Most of us are not good listeners. Listening takes practice. It's been said that the difference between a successful career and a mediocre one sometimes consists of leaving about four to five things a day unsaid. In other words, work on your listening skills.

You don't have to be an extrovert to be successful in networking. Shy people are often better networkers just because they appear to be better listeners. But listening involves much more than keeping our mouths shut.

Eighty-five percent of your career success is dependent on your communications skills and forty-five percent of those skills have to do with body language. How approachable are you? Do you smile at others? Is your smile sincere and warm, or does it look like it's pasted on? Are you maintaining eye contact when someone is talking with you? If you glance away for a split second you'll insult the person you're talking with. If you stare at the other person, you may be perceived as bored or even condescending. So don't forget to blink!

Hot Tip!

If someone mentions a family member or even a pet, the next question out of your mouth should always be "What's his or her name?" Here's an example. Let's say the person you're chatting with says, my daughter's leaving for college this weekend. Ask, "What's your daughter's name?" That simple question surprises and delights most people because it's not expected.

If her name is Emily, then ask, "How old is Emily?"

"Which college will she be attending?"

"How did she select that college?"

Continue to use Emily's name at appropriate times during the rest of conversation. You have just created a powerful follow-up tool. Now, instead of offering your business card, ASK for theirs. Then say, "Good luck moving Emily up to college."

Connection Tool 4:
Know Your Commercial

You're networking at a big event and a prospective client asks, "What do you do?" Watch his eyes glaze over when you answer, "I'm a consultant," or "I sell widgets." No matter what your profession, you only have about thirty seconds to spark enough interest to give you an opportunity to tell that person about the benefits of what you do.

Develop a personal commercial that will intrigue people when they ask about your business.

Which do you think will generate interest for an insurance agent — "I sell life insurance" or "I help people protect their family's future."

Instead of telling people that I'm a speaker, trainer, or consultant, I say, "I help people boost their profits by increasing customer loyalty." If I really want to get someone's attention, I say "I help CEO's sleep at night." I guarantee you they always ask me how! Now that I've aroused their curiosity, I can tell them how my services can boost their profits without it sounding like a sales pitch!

Create your own 30-second commercial. Brainstorm with colleagues and friends to help you develop a short, memorable statement that tells people how you benefit them. Make sure it's easy for others to repeat.

Connection Tool 5:
Stay Connected

Create a list of your top twenty contacts and make an effort to touch base with them at least once a quarter. Be sure to include past clients and hot prospects, plus everyone who has ever made a referral to your business or sung your praises. This project can be accomplished through a newsletter, e-mail "tip of the month," phone call, birthday card, fax, or a hand-written note attached to an article that may be of interest or value to them.

Your reasons for staying in touch should not always be business related: Make sure you provide value whenever you send out any kind of information. If you have actively listened to others, you'll have lots of creative ideas for ways to follow-up.

One way that I stay in touch with my clients and prospects is by sending them a free e-mail newsletter or e-zine twice a month. It includes tips and articles chock full of information to help them build customer loyalty, boost sales, retain employees, and grow professionally.

Connection Tool 6: Follow-up

If you have promised anyone anything — a business contact, the name of a vendor, directions to a golf course, or even your mom's chicken soup recipe — follow-up as soon as possible. How many times have people told you they're going to send you information or give you a call and then you never hear from them? Did you forget about their offer? Probably not, and you'll be less inclined to do business with them because their lack of follow-up may be a reflection of how they conduct their business.

While flying home from Atlanta, I began chatting with the gentleman seated next to me on the airplane. He told me he and his family had just moved to Milwaukee from Washington, DC. Before I discussed any business with him, I asked how many children he had, their names, and ages. He loved telling me all about Megan and Katie.

Then, I asked him about the company he worked for and his role in that company. It turns out that he's vice president of North American sales for his company, and he has a need for sales training. We exchanged business cards.

When I sent him a package of information about my business and sales training, I included a magazine called *Metro Parent*, which is loaded with resources and information on things to do with your family in our community. I attached a handwritten note that simply said, "This magazine will give you lots of ideas for fun things to do with Megan and Katie!"

Every interaction you have is an opportunity to either build or destroy your personal credibility. Follow-up as fast as possible on every commitment you make — no matter how small or insignificant it may seem at the time.

Any time someone sends you a business lead or gives you a great idea, send back a *hand-written* thank you note. Never include your business card with the note or you will dilute the sincerity of your message.

Connection Tool 7: Volunteer

Your most powerful networking tool of all is volunteering. It evens the playing field. When you serve on nonprofit committees and boards, socio-economic barriers are removed. Instead, you all become volunteers who care about kids or hunger, or whatever the cause may be.

But here's the catch. Never join a board or committee unless you sincerely believe in the cause and you intend to treat your commitment as a job. We all know people who volunteer and then never show up for the meetings or fail to follow-through on their assignments. Just as a stellar volunteer track record can build your credibility and your career, a dismal track record can destroy your reputation.

Don't expect to step onto high-powered boards unless you are a CEO of a major corporation or very wealthy. Volunteerism is the same as building a career. You take it one step at a time, by serving on a committee or organizing a special event. If you've handled yourself professionally and with integrity, you'll be recognized and invited to move up the volunteer ladder. I was asked to serve on the most powerful nonprofit board in Milwaukee only after I had already served as a volunteer for thirteen years in many other capacities. I had to pay my dues first.

Connection Tool 8:
Keep Track of the Details

If you don't keep track of the details someone has shared with you during the course of a conversation, you have missed a powerful opportunity to build a long-term relationship. Write them down. When you're chatting with someone and she mentions her son's name and the college he'll be attending, the first thing you should do *after* you walk away is write it down. Cocktail napkins or the backs of my business cards are handy tools. Update your contact files the minute you return to your office. You will not be able to master networking if you don't maintain your contact files.

ACT 2000 and Microsoft Outlook are excellent computer database programs, but there are many more on the market. The important thing is to select a method of managing information and use it consistently.

First, enter the basic business card information. Next, enter the *important* information. Be sure to note the date and nature of your first or last contact with that person. List names of his or her associates. Include the person's primary areas of expertise and special interests. Include information about any community activities the person is involved in, business goals, personal goals, family information, and memberships.

It's been said that successful people are only three handshakes away from their next sale. When you apply these power tools to master the art of networking, you can be sure business will grow beyond your wildest dreams.

Remember this old Irish Proverb —"Don't ever slam the door. Some day you might want to get back in."

About
Debra J. Schmidt, M.S.

*D*ebra J. Schmidt, a.k.a. "The Loyalty Builder," is the owner of Spectrum Consulting Group Inc. based in Milwaukee, WI. She works with people who want to grow their business by helping them build customer loyalty, boost sales and develop powerful marketing strategies. Her extensive client list includes Northwestern Mutual, Kohler Co. and the Green Bay Packers. Emmy nominee, entrepreneur, television personality and winner of six national marketing awards, Debra is one of the nation's top business consultants and speakers. She is also the author of 101 Ways to Build Customer Loyalty. *To check out the complete selection of Loyalty Builder products, subscribe to Debra Schmidt's FREE email newsletter, and get hundreds of tips on how to grow YOUR business. For information on training and consulting, or to book Debra J. Schmidt as a speaker for your next event, visit: www.SpectrumResults.com*

Contact Information:
Debra J. Schmidt, M.S.
Spectrum Consulting Group Inc.
P.O. Box 170954
Milwaukee, WI 53217-8086
Phone: (414) 964-3872
Fax: (414) 967-0875
E-mail: deb@theloyaltybuilder.com
Website: www.SpectrumResults.com

Your Price is Too High!

by Al Tetrault, M.B.A.

Every salesperson and many others within selling organizations have heard this lament. Whether at the start of the sales process, or as a final objection to closing the sale, the prospect says, "Your price is too high." Now, the selling *really* begins!

The successful salesperson learns to respond to this inevitable objection. Even the prospect who is ready to buy will present the price objection to obtain a discount. Knowledgeable buyers know that there is often a standard discount for which they qualify. For example, when checking into a hotel, the smart buyer will ask if this is the best price while signing the registry, knowing that this question will likely lead to a discount as a result of AAA, AARP, AOPA, USAA or some other organization. Often, the desk clerk has discount authority, and simply asking will result in a lower rate.

In business-to-business transactions, the price objection is often a request for more information to defend the purchase and is, therefore, an opportunity to sell the value of the product or service. This justification may be to satisfy senior management or the buyer's own sense of getting the best possible price. *The danger is to respond to the wrong price objection.*

Six Basic Price Objections

There are six fundamental perspectives regarding price:

- Price versus competition

- Price versus approved budget

- Price versus buyer expectations

- Price versus a process alternative

- Price versus a percentage of the product price (for continuing services)

- Price versus "do-it-yourself"

Each perspective must be understood, and the sales response to each should reflect that understanding. Responding to a price objection that does not currently exist in the prospect's mind may simply raise that specific objection unnecessarily.

When faced with a price objection, the first challenge is to learn precisely which price objection is relevant. The best approach to the objection is simply to ask questions to further refine the prospect's perception. One of my favorite responses to this query is simply "Oh?" The phrases "Tell me more" or "Explain," will usually elicit the information needed to respond positively to the price objection.

Price versus Competition

The most common assertion you're likely to hear in the marketplace is that your price is too high compared to competition. Assuming that the marketing organization has properly priced the product or service, the challenge now is to discover the differences between what's being offered by the competitor and your proposal. Frequently, the competition's price is lower because the product or service is less robust. Sometimes, it is related to a time-specific "special offer." In either case, there is now enough information to respond positively to the objection: "Your price is too high!"

Consider this scenario. A company is exploring the purchase and installation of an Enterprise Resource Planning (ERP) system. Several software providers have been invited to prepare and present a proposal. After several meetings between the software manufacturers and various users within the company, the proposals are received and reviewed by the purchasing committee. Your proposal calls for a software license of $150,000 and additional installation and support services of $150,000, for a total initial cost of $300,000. Annual maintenance cost is $30,000 for this solution. The competition's proposal is for a software license of $100,000 and additional installation and support services of $150,000, for a total initial cost of $250,000. They also propose annual maintenance cost of $30,000. The competitor's proposal appears to be less expensive by $50,000.

The information systems manager reviews the proposals in detail. He discovers that your proposal includes modules to connect your multi-plant locations, and the installation and support services for these modules and the annual maintenance fees are included in the base proposal. The competition has not included these modules in their proposal, proposing to install these modules later at additional cost. The additional cost will be $30,000 plus $30,000 of professional services and an additional annual maintenance cost of $3,000. Analysis of the proposal, in detail, shows that the functionality between offerings is significant. Your price is higher than the competition, but it is more comprehensive and elegant in addressing the issues discovered during the sales process.

Further discussion with the prospect reveals these discrepancies. Now, you can either reduce your product offering to meet the competitor's price or show the enhanced value of your proposal to the prospect. Either approach will likely lead to an elimination of price as a valid objection.

Price versus Approved Budget

Sometimes a client develops a budget based on old or unreliable data. If the prospect learned about your company through word of mouth, she may have been told about a less expensive solution provided by your company to a friend. Her situation, however, may require a more expensive solution. If a budget was established based on the friend's solution, then this situation needs to be explored. This process will result in reducing the proposed solution or acceptance of the higher price for the original solution. In either case, the key to responding to the price objection is to ask questions and gain more information.

Probing questions will reveal how the prospect established the budget. If the basis was inadequate data, there is an opportunity to address the issue of value you are providing. Value is based on three propositions:

- Your proposed solution will increase revenue for the firm.
- Your proposed solution will reduce costs.
- Your proposed solution will avoid additional costs in the future.

Each of these basic propositions may be present in your sales situation, and there may be the added psychological buying needs of status, image, and similar intangibles. The important concept to keep in focus is the need to determine how the budget was developed and to provide additional information that increases the value as well as the budget. If this objective cannot be met, then the challenge is to reduce the scope of the proposed solution to fit into the approved budget.

Price versus Buyer Expectations

Price expectations are often unrelated to value or competition but are simply an intuitive feel for what a product or service should cost. This can be a difficult objection, since the perception must be addressed, and it may be cultural or psychological, and unrelated to value.

Travel is a case in point. Prices for all goods and services are considerably higher in Japan and Paris than in the United States. Most travelers have difficulty accepting these high prices, and you will often hear people complain about these prices and vow never to return to those places again.

When selling business services in this situation, you might need to introduce the marketplace to validate the prices. Pointing out that your prices are competitive with other products or service providers, although risking introducing a competitor, is the only recourse. When this step is necessary, the strategy is to provide pricing relative to competitors whose higher prices or lower quality are well known in the marketplace, and against whom you compete very effectively.

Price versus a Process Alternative

There is often a process alternative for the prospect, and your price is being compared to that situation. Buying computer software to do a task may be compared to a manual method. This type of situation is common in business when a system is already in place, such as a customer service department, and a new solution is being proposed (CRM) which will alter the basic business process and produce benefits in addition to higher costs.

Once again, the key to success in overcoming the price objection is to explain and demonstrate the additional value of the proposed solution. In the example cited, the new CRM solution will perform new tasks that are not currently being implemented. The impact of this enhanced service may be a higher price. Probing questions will reveal the potential for increased revenue and profits as a result of a higher level of service to the customer. The system will also likely avoid the higher costs that occur when the additional tasks are not performed. For example, post installation and warranty communications will not only increase customer satisfaction, but also identify problems early in the life cycle of the product or service. Early identification will lead to early resolution and a delighted customer who will be a stronger reference account for your firm. Quantifying these data will overcome the objection of the higher price by demonstrating the greater value.

Price versus a Percentage of the Product Price (for continuing services)

Sometimes the maintenance or continuing support costs become greater than the original cost of the product. Two decades ago, computer hardware and software were significantly more expensive than the continuing support costs. Today, with the reduction in the cost and the increase in power of both hardware and software, and the simultaneous increase in the cost of labor, this relationship has changed. In addition, support today may be more comprehensive than it was in the past for the same products. Questions and information can relate these changes to the prospect and disarm the price objection.

When the cost of continuing warranty support exceeds 10 percent of the initial cost of the product, there is likely to be price resistance. This is an important marketing issue, and the product-pricing decision makers will balance these factors when creating the product-marketing plan. A higher initial price will impede the initial sale while a lower initial price will help to sell the product. The trade-off is the continuing warranty and support cost. If it is too high, the customers will not commit to service, and the result will be customer satisfaction issues in the event of future problems. If the cost is too low, it will be difficult to provide continuing quality support on a subsidized basis. There are many variables that can impact the cost of continuing support services, and they are not all within the supplier's control.

If the price objection is heard with respect to continuing services after the warranty period, then an approach that could be explored is that of the total cost of ownership. Using the timeframe of the normal life cycle of the product, add the initial cost plus the continuing cost for the term of the product life cycle. Then, use this calculation to relate to the value of the product or service.

Another consideration here is the customer's own accounting system. Sometimes the initial cost is capitalized and depreciated as an asset, and the continuing warranty and service costs are expensed as incurred during the operating period. The prospect may have limited flexibility with the operating budget and more options with the capital equipment budget. This case would suggest bundling the continuing costs into the initial costs and providing no additional cost warranty for the life cycle of the product. These options are dependent upon accurately identifying the relevant price objection.

Price versus "Do-it-Yourself"

The comparison of the price versus "do-it-yourself" often denies the cost of labor of the participant and the extended time involved for a person to accomplish the proposed solution. A simple example is lawn care. Certainly everyone can do this task at less expense than an outside service, yet few persons enjoy spending time on this chore. Those who choose to do it themselves place less value on their time, or truly enjoy this activity, than those who contract their lawn maintenance.

In selling to the education marketplace, and especially the universities, this is a difficult price objection. The university often directs graduate students to perform tasks that they are able to accomplish but that are not the best use of their time and talent. Yet, their services are "free" to the university. If the graduate student could be performing other work, which would provide income to the university, this approach to demonstrating value might be a solution.

Another situation, which is perhaps easier to address, is in the commercial environment. If a prospect indicates that she can "do-it-herself," the challenge is to help her understand the value of her time. Then, you can compare the value of her time used to perform the task with the price of the service you've proposed.

In the simple example noted earlier, the business executive or sales representative who spends time on lawn maintenance can be approached logically. The first step is to evaluate the professional's time. It is likely that this professional's time is valued at more than $50 per hour. The time required by the professional to perform this task is four hours per week. The cost of the lawn service is much less than $200 per week. So, if the professional can employ himself for these four hours on productive tasks, there is a net advantage to outsourcing the lawn maintenance task. In addition, there are psychic rewards for the professional who does not enjoy lawn maintenance chores.

Summary

Every salesperson will regularly be confronted with the statement: "Your price is too high!" Then, selling begins. The challenge is to gain additional information through questioning, identifying the appropriate price objection, and responding with information supporting the quoted price. A rush to confront the price objection risks responding incorrectly, and thereby introducing another and different price objection.

About
Al Tetrault, M.B.A.

*A*lbert R. Tetrault is Chairman of the Innovative Strategies Group, a Management Consulting firm. His business experience and expertise is in helping companies develop and implement plans for revenue growth and profitability, including the development of sales, marketing, financial and operation plans. Al has successfully led the turnaround of three companies as CEO. Earlier in his career, he served IBM and Digital Equipment Corporation in sales, marketing and operations management, domestically and internationally. He served in the USAF as an aircraft commander of C-130s. A Vietnam Veteran, he earned the Bronze Star and several Air Medals. Al earned an M.B.A. (cum laude) at the Harvard Business School and a B.A. in Economics at the University of Connecticut. He has studied international business at the London Business School and IMEDE in Lausanne, Switzerland. Al serves on the Board of Directors of the Society of International Business Fellows, the Harvard Business School Club and Electronic Commerce Systems He is a member of the National Association of Corporate Directors and is a former member of the Business and Technology Alliance serving on the Board of Directors in 1993-1994.

Contact Information:
Albert R. Tetrault, M.B.A.
Chairman, Innovative Strategies Group
P.O. Box 76551
Atlanta, GA 30358
Phone: (770) 310-3175
Fax: (877) 471-1387
E-mail: tetrault@revenue-growth.com
Website: www.revenue-growth.com

ROOM4$

by Mary E. Cremeans, M.B.A.

So the reason you bought this book was to find tips, tools, and inspiration to help you become more successful, faster. This chapter will provide you with some special tips and tools that Information Technology (IT) professionals have used for years, but few salespeople have ever heard of. Whether you have a brand new concept that you are trying to launch or have been running your sales activity for some time, you have the chance to increase your sales in any economy using the proven resources found here to add to your business success. You already know the basics of sales and how to close the deal, but what you may not know is how to organize yourself and analyze your situation to make the best decisions for process change. You know the old saying, "If you always do what you always did, you will always get what you always got." If you are tired of getting what you always got, it's time for change! It's time to make ROOM4$.

As I look back on my sales career, I can't believe I have survived. I was so gullible. I took excess risk. I didn't heed common sense and the basics. I needed to learn how to get my act together! I didn't know what was essential or important. Then I learned from the experts in the IT field. The IT industry has been fiercely competitive over the last decade. In order to survive, the workers in this industry have developed tools to help them produce faster, better, cheaper. These tools help them make change more easily and allow continuous process improvement. The only way to effect change is to alter the process. There are no shortcuts. Do you want to focus on performing faster, better, and at less cost to yourself?

The Art and Process of Making Room4$

When we buy a new piece of furniture, we have to make room for it. When we have a new baby or Granny comes to live with us, we have to make room for them. We are used to making room for things in our life, but we are not used to the concept of making room for more success and more money in our lives. We have room in our lives for everything we want. However, we don't have room for everything. All of the excess becomes a distraction, and we easily lose focus on what we are doing. So, how do we decide what we will have room for? First, we need to know what our vision and mission are. These are the "why" and "what" behind our doing. I won't get into detailed vision and mission statement creation here because there are books written solely for that purpose. However, what I want to emphasize is that your first, foremost, and primary need is to focus.

You say you want to be more successful, and you want success quickly. Well, you can't achieve it without focus. To make room for more, you have to eliminate the extras in your life that interfere with your focus. Your end goal has to be crystal clear. You have to know what you are shooting for. In the IT industry, there are two methods of software development that require rigid structure. One of these was developed for the United States Department of Defense. Both methodologies require that the Mission Statement be memorized by everyone on the project team. When auditors perform interviews, individuals on the team are expected to recite their Mission Statement. Can you do that in your own sales business? If you go to a Toastmasters Club meeting or to a Rotary Club meeting, you will often hear them recite their Mission Statement.

When was the last time you stopped to think about why you are in this particular sales position? What was your vision when you accepted this role? What was your driving force? Perhaps this was a means for added income, or perhaps it was an avenue for financial freedom or even personal freedom from the daily "clocking in at work." Or, perhaps you were trying to help out a friend by jumping on board. Now, if it was the latter, perhaps your mission was accomplished. More likely, however, you had a vision of some sort that would help you eliminate some of the "pain" in your life at that time. If that's the case, has any of that pain been eliminated (be it debt, or unemployment, or whatever)? Have you realized any benefit or gain?

If the answer is yes, then some positive change has occurred, and your vision and mission were probably on track. If the answer is no, then we have to analyze why not. Was the vision really yours? Or, was it someone else's dream for you? If you truly own your vision and mission for your sales position, there is nothing that can keep you from success.

When I was working toward my M.B.A., I worked endlessly on corporate business cases. I noticed that all of these companies had a Vision Statement and a Mission Statement. I decided that I, too, needed to give my life some direction, so I created my own personal Vision Statement. My Vision Statement became "Help others to grow." I wanted something to put on my tombstone, so when it was all said and done, I would have no regrets. I look to the future, and hope to have inscribed on my tombstone "She helped others to grow." At that time, my family and friends will be my only testament, and I don't want to fail the words chiseled into the stone that my grandchildren will read. I think of that tombstone often, and that helps me keep my vision and my focus.

Exercise 1: Complete your Vision Statement and Mission Statement here. If you can't do it, refer to your library for books on this specific topic (hundreds are available).

Write your Vision here:

_____

_____

_____

Write your Mission here:

_____

_____

_____

Once you have your Vision and Mission Statements recorded, memorize them, and be able to share them with anyone who asks.

Tip 1: Part of making room for more success is defining a focal point to help you weed out unnecessary distractions that will inhibit your success. Create your Vision and Mission Statements first.

You say, "OK, but . . ." All right, you are a lone salesperson, and nobody else will ever ask. Q: Do you need to document them in writing anyway? A: Yes! If you can't do this, you are not serious about making room for more success. This will help you focus.

Getting the Right Start (Easy As P-L-A-N)

Once you have completed your Vision and Mission Statements, you are ready to begin with your Plan. All major IT companies have professional project managers. One of their primary roles and functions is to develop a Plan. Auditors review the Plan to ensure it includes all of the necessary elements. You may be thinking that this is just too much for you, but let's put it in perspective. If you go on a picnic, don't you have to do some planning? You have to plan what food to take (and how much, so everyone is fed), when and where you plan to go, and the setup for your picnic (i.e., Do you need a grill or is there one at the park?).

Plans can be very simple, or they can be complex. What you need to do is make a plan to match what you are trying to do. Scale it to fit your needs. I remember one woman who set up such a rigorous plan for her picnic, she never went. It was too much trouble. She overlooked her vision (creating childhood memories for her kids) and her mission (to enjoy shared family time). I took a lesson from her. When I want to take my child to the park, I will dump some packaged cookies in a bag, toss in some peanut butter sandwiches, then grab a bottle of water or soda. We go! No, we don't have an elaborate grilled meal, but we meet our objectives of creating childhood memories and enjoying shared family time.

P — Picture what you are trying to do, and put your objectives into words (on paper).

L — List everyone involved and their responsibilities; then share all of this information.

A — Adjust as needed (i.e., If it rains on your picnic, what is your alternative?).

N — Name your milestones, your measures, your needs, your risks, and your prize.

I was once on a task force headed by Joanne. I was greatly impressed by her ability to prepare everyone in the group quickly so that the ramp-up time was minimal and implementation was a sure success. I remarked to her about her skills and ability, and she shrugged them off as no big deal. She said she had been in so many task force groups that she had developed a template that she used all the time. The beauty of this template is that it can be easily duplicated by anyone.

I. Start with a three-ring binder thick enough to handle anticipated documents (minimum 1").

II. Insert preprinted colored tabs numbered 1-10.

III. Make a Table of Contents (using the sheet from the preprinted tabs package) listing these ten items.

1. Mission Statement

2. Contact List (names, phone numbers, addresses with zip codes, e-mail addresses, fax numbers, cell phone numbers)

3. Organization (announcements and organization chart)

4. Background (presentation material such as PowerPoint slides or Word documents)

5. Charter (Summary of tasks including: Vision Statement, objectives, and goals)

6. Things to Do (calendar of meetings/events, weekly schedule, and other*)

7. Historic Reference Articles (e-mails, policies, standards)

8. Roles and Responsibilities (narrative explanation)

9. Final Report (Coordinator Summary and Members' Progress Chart)

10. Appendices: Glossary of Terms, Blank Notes Pages

*Make up checklists of meeting materials that are needed for each meeting (i.e., flip charts, markers, tape, etc.) and food ordering info (i.e., pizza place information and pricing info, or cafeteria contact and food items).

IV. Prepare the documents for each section, and put your binder(s) together.

Exercise 2: Complete your Plan. At a minimum, use the three-ring binder format with the ten numbered sections, or use another format (which includes all of those basic items). If you have more time, energy, and money, or if you have greater risk, you may want to use a business plan software package that will help you drill down to more detail. If you have a team working with you, delegate the various sections out, if you can, with deadlines for getting the information completed and returned. Make sure you follow the journalist's rule, answering the *who, what, when, where, why, how,* and *how much* questions.

Once you have your plan (the entire notebook and all sections completed), duplicate the notebook for everyone who works with you. Schedule a formal meeting and review it together. Everyone on your team will be ready to roll.

Tip 2: Remember the basic elements of the P-L-A-N:

P — Picture what you are trying to do, and put your objectives into words (and on paper).

L — List persons involved and their responsibilities; then share all of this information.

A — Adjust as needed (i.e., If it rains on your picnic, what is your alternative?)

N — Name your milestones, your measures, your needs, your risks, and your prize.

You say, "OK, but . . ." All right, you are a lone salesperson, and nobody else is involved. Q: Do you need to document your Plan in writing anyway, making this notebook (at minimum)? A: Yes! If you can't do this, you are not serious about making room for more success. Now if you have this information in another format, that's OK, as long as you have all of the ingredients. You need to make sure your Contacts information is all in the same place and that you have complete details (i.e., zip codes). If you aren't proficient on the PC, enlist the help of a friend or professional assistant to help you pull this information together if you don't want handwritten material. The act of putting this document together will help you analyze resources (people, finances, and equipment), risk, schedule, and much more. When you start outlining tasks and milestones, and putting dates on a calendar, your Vision starts to take shape, and your Mission begins to fall into place. Your end goal is much clearer.

You say, "Yes, but . . ." All right, your manager or up line says you don't need to bother with all of this; just hit the streets and get going. If you have your Vision (your dream) that's all you need. I have to argue with that. If you don't make room for baby or Granny when they come into your home, you will end up with a mess on your hands in no time. Every person and every project has to have "room" to be functional and effective. Trying to hang everything on the dream alone won't work. You need to have some form of infrastructure to sustain you.

One time I was being driven by a manager who insisted I invest in certain materials. I didn't have a plan, and I bought into my manager's advice without considering my available resources.

When I did a review of my results, I was shocked at how much I had invested in an area that provided no payback. I was gullible. Don't you make the same mistake. I had told this manager I needed to get organized and needed help, and he told me that was my problem. I didn't need more material; I needed more training. True, I had to take the responsibility, but I needed to know what the essential and the important issues were. People need information in a useful format. Don't ignore the basic needs for planning what is needed. A plan will help you think through every aspect of your endeavor. It will help you reduce risk and produce positive results faster.

Planning helps define your "on-time" and "off-time." Did you know that highly successful people make time to work hard and play hard? If you have your work clearly defined, you can work hard at it, and then you will have time to play. If not, your work will spill over into your family and personal life. Your objectives will blur, and you will become ineffective. Take time to plan!

Preparing Your Toolkit

Here is where the rubber meets the road. If you were a doctor, you would have certain items in your medical bag. Doctors have the basic necessities to help meet our physical needs. The same is true of a carpenter. Carpenters have the basic tools required to get the job done. A salesman doesn't repair things, but he still needs tools. You need to have tools that help you make more sales and to track and analyze your success. You need tools to help define 1) what needs to be done, and 2) what needs to be changed. Do you have a toolkit? If not, here are some handy tools to include:

Decomposition Quality Analysis (DQA) sheets, Checklists, and Fishbone Diagram sheets. There are many other tools, but these are all simple and easy to implement.

Decomposition Quality Analysis (DQA) sheets are used to define your processes.

Checklists are used to help you quickly and accurately complete recurring tasks.

Fishbone Diagrams are used to clearly identify problem areas for correction.

Decomposition Quality Analysis (DQA) sheets were originated by IBM. They help you decompose your processes to the bare bones. You start by taking a blank sheet, and filling in the *middle* column with VERBS that describe your process activity. Then you complete the other columns with stakeholder and input/output. Here's an example of a high level DQA.

You can take each process row and break it down even further on a page by itself. For starters, just use the high-level DQA. Remember to start with the middle column, using verbs to describe the process. This tool will help you identify what resources you need to perform a task as well as what output you should have when you are finished.

Decomposition Quality Analysis (DQA) Sheet

Stakeholder (FROM)	Input	Process	Output	Stakeholder (TO)
Customer request for information	• Customer contact card • Flip chart • Markers • Sales literature • Blank applications	Makes sales presentation and close	• Completed flip charts • Completed application • Signed contract • Updated customer contact card • Check for deposit	Manager or up line receives check, application and other updates
New Associate requests training	• Training manual • Audio tapes • Video tapes • Flip chart • Markers • Tape • Sales literature • Blank applications • Customer contact cards • Blank training certificate	Train new Associate	• Certificate of training completion for Associate • Notice of training completion • Completed flip charts	Manager or up line receives notice of training completion Associate receives training certificate

Checklists (check sheets) take many forms. Once you have completed your DQA sheet, you could create custom check sheets from the input and output columns. For instance, when you prepare to train a new associate, you know you need to have all of the materials gathered in the Input column. To ensure you have completed your tasks, your checklist could include all of the Output column items. You don't have to create a DQA to make checklists. Earlier I mentioned using the journalist's questions when you create your plan. That is a form of checklist. I also mentioned using a checklist to order food for meetings. Checklists are an easy and effective tool to develop and use. They relieve you from the burden of having to remember everything all the time. Checklists help you complete your job fast and accurately. It costs more in time and energy to go back to correct things than it does to do them right the first time. Use checklists to do your job completely and correctly the first time. If you are in a sales business that requires many forms (such as insurance sales), having a checklist will help you prepare to have everything you need when you close, including reminders to sign certain documents. It is much easier to check items off your checklist than it is to go back to the customer with the form.

Fishbone Diagrams help you determine where to focus your energies when you are plagued with nagging problems. The head of the "fish" includes the problem statement. The "bones" of the fish are labeled with various resource or process items (i.e., people, plant, process, material). You can use additional or other labels that may be more meaningful. Once you have your diagram, brainstorm potential causes for the problem you are trying to solve and write them next to the bone for the category they fall under.

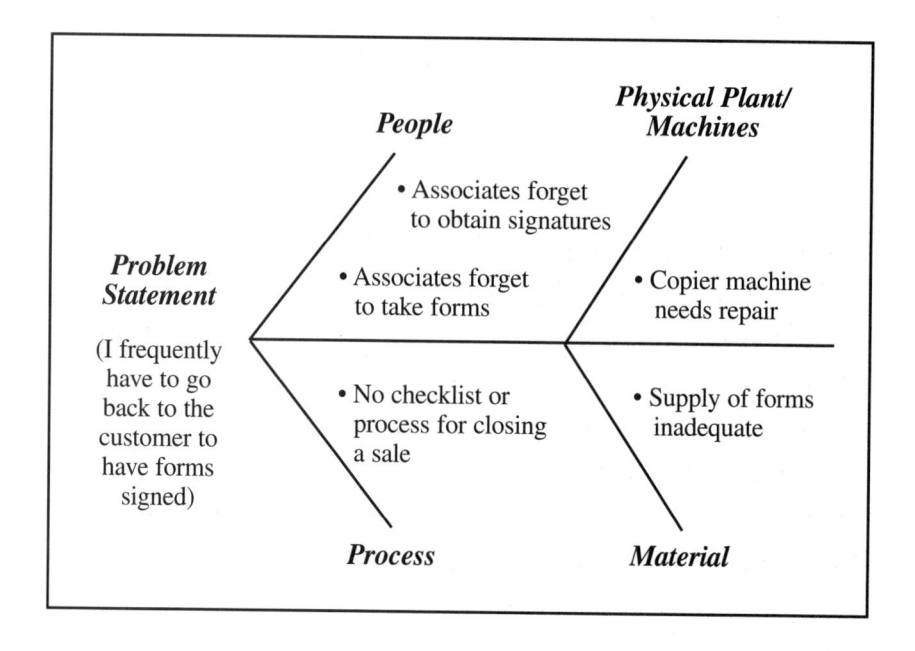

```
                    People          Physical Plant/
                                      Machines
                      • Associates forget
                        to obtain signatures
  Problem
  Statement          • Associates forget    • Copier machine
                      to take forms          needs repair
  (I frequently
  have to go
  back to the        • No checklist or      • Supply of forms
  customer to         process for closing    inadequate
  have forms          a sale
  signed)

                       Process              Material
```

Most of the time one of the "bones" will fill up with more causes than the others do. This will indicate where most of your problems are. Sometimes you may want to tackle that bone, or you may want to tackle a bone that will result in a "quick hit" for problem resolution. This tool is effective for solving problems in a non-emotional way. It is used best in a group setting in which the group gets to brainstorm the causes, but it can also be used by one person.

Exercise 3: Complete a DQA for one of your processes. You can draw the form on a blank sheet of paper, or you can write it on a chalkboard or flip chart. You probably have many processes. Just start asking yourself, "What do you do?" Start with the middle PROCESS column using VERBS to describe what you do. Once you get the hang of it, you will need to record all of your processes.

Provider	Input	Process	Output	Recipient

Tip 3: Part of making room for more success is clearly defining what you do and how you do it (defining your processes and procedures).

You say, "OK, but . . ." All right, you work by yourself, and you think this is overkill. Working by yourself may be all the more reason to use these tools. They can quickly show you where you need to add resources.

Opening the Door on your Room4$

Now that you know how the process works, and you have a toolkit that equips you for your everyday sales demands, it's time for you to make ROOM4$, and get started. Open the door for more, and start using these techniques, tips, and tools.

About
Mary E. Cremeans, M.B.A.

Mary Cremeans is a consultant, writer, trainer and implementation specialist who works with individuals and organizations that want to improve their current situation to make room for a better future. Mary's professional background includes extensive experience in the Information Technology (IT) industry as well as in finance/accounting and insurance. This unique combination of experiences gives her the precise tools necessary to work with those in search of personal, financial, and corporate business direction. Many have relied on Mary's expertise and guidance in the areas of insight management, financial planning, transition, systems and quality analysis, and process strategies. Mary is a member of the National Speakers Association where she is also a member of the Professional Expert Groups (PEGs) for: Technology, and Writers and Publishers.

Contact Information:
Mary E. Cremeans, M.B.A.
A&P Group
15580 Oakcrest Circle
Brooksville, FL 34604-8238
Phone: (352) 796-6880
E-mail: shopkeep@quixnet.net

Understanding Your Customer

by Sara Owens

Think about previous sales calls that you have made. Have you ever been in a selling situation and thought to yourself, "Why isn't my prospective customer responding?" You find yourself looking at faces covered with blank stares. As you painfully inch your way through the remainder of your presentation, you realize that you have not connected with your prospect at all. The likelihood of a sale is minimal.

So, you go back to your office and ponder, "What did I do wrong? What does my target customer want? I don't think I'll ever understand him/her/them."

And that's where I can help. I was your prospect for more than a decade. I worked for the largest (Kraft Foods) and second-largest (ConAgra Foods) food companies in the United States. I influenced or controlled budgets close to 100 million dollars. I bought a lot of goods and services. I was approached during this time by many sales "professionals." Some had not earned the right to be called professional. The differentiating factor for those sales people I ended up working with was whether they understood my business and wanted to help me grow it. It was obvious that some were in my office only to "sell me," not help me.

As a prospective customer I do not like the feeling of "being sold." Certain salespeople were known for wanting only to line their own pockets with commissions. I felt as though these "professionals" would sell me a tutu to wear to a funeral and then assure me that it was the absolutely perfect outfit for the occasion. In addition, they would ask if I wanted tap shoes to wear with my tutu.

I like to think of myself as an intelligent woman. When a salesperson tells me something I believe to be fundamentally untrue, I think this person is treating me like I am not intelligent. As a prospective customer, I want to hear the truth. Perhaps those salespersons in my past believed they could help my company. But, if so, it was not clear to me. The connection was not made.

Time and time again, I have wished that the people who were selling to me would, could understand me. I have wished the focus were on what could be done for *me*, not on what could be done for them. Whether it was someone in my office looking for approval for a potential program, or someone externally looking for a sale, I was ultimately interested in only three things:

- Will it move more volume?
- Will it generate more profit?
- Will it increase my share?

In short, I was interested in "making my numbers." "Making my numbers" is business shorthand for the goals that management agrees to make at the beginning of every fiscal year. These numbers typically are Volume, Profit and Share. Different companies call measures different names, but all desire what they represent.

Volume

Volume is the first priority for a company. Related directly to the top-line, volume is how much you sell. Whether it is a service or a product, whether it's measured in projects, liters, pounds or units, without volume there is no influx of cash. Volume is my term (and many others) for "what comes in."

Volume is critical for companies. When volume grows, profit follows. More money *in* equals more money *out*. As volume increases, there are more funds available for investment; plants run more efficiently; fixed costs are spread across more units, thereby lowering cost per unit; the impact of cost-savings that have been put in place multiply, and distributors are happy to spend time and effort selling for you.

Just as a salesperson was interested in making a sale to me, I was interested in making sales to my customers.

Profit

Profit is also the first priority for a company. As a customer I learned to prioritize very well. Why settle for only one first priority when there are so many to choose from?

The dot-com companies in the late 1990's existed solely to create volume, assuming profit would follow. These dot-com companies, for the most part, no longer exist. Most companies with dreams of longevity pursue profit — aggressively at that.

The Dow Jones Average rose from 2,634 at the end of 1990 to 10,787 at the end of 2000. United States business enjoyed a decade of extraordinary growth. Investors became wealthier, and expectations for all companies rose. Memories of the good times have not faded after our brief recession, nor have expectations. It is not enough for a company to deliver one or two percent profit growth per year. Most companies are aiming for double-digit growth. Or at least five to ten percent profit growth.

Volume fuels the top-line and profit is what remains on the bottom-line. Growing volume is definitely the most pleasant, sustainable, and healthy way to grow profit. Unfortunately, it is increasingly difficult to move more volume and generate consistent profit growth. Sometimes companies focus on taking costs out of the system. You are familiar, I'm sure, with this concept. Price is a big factor in sales today. There are a number of issues to consider.

Issue 1: The population of the United States is growing at less than two percent a year. Per the latest Census, the population grew 13.2 percent from 1990 to 2000. This equates to a compound annual growth rate of 1.2 percent. Sales of goods or services change proportionately with the population. They grow as the number of people increases. Assuming "status quo," a company could expect to grow volume, or sales, only 1.2 percent based on the fact that it would have only 1.2 percent more users each year.

Issue 2: Multiple brands or services are perceived to be alike. Fewer brands, companies, or services are perceived to be significantly better than their competitors. Instead these brands are viewed as being interchangeable. People are equally satisfied (or dissatisfied) with Hertz and Avis, or Tide and Cheer, or Keebler and

Nabisco. Instead of being loyal to one brand, consumers are loyal to a set of brands.

In this scenario, brands are perceived to be of equal value, and, therefore, consumers purchase the brand with the lowest price. As you can imagine, competing on price is not conducive to healthy profit margins.

Issue 3: Retailer consolidation and power shift. In the case of consumer-packaged goods, there has been a significant power shift over the past twenty years from the manufacturer to the retailer. In the past, manufacturers produced many important brands and retail customers would complain if key brands were missing. Today, a handful of retailers control more than half of all goods sold, and a manufacturer who is not stocked in these accounts misses out on a huge amount of sales. As the retailer gains power, more marketing dollars are funneled to the retailer and more emphasis placed on immediate volume gained by trade spending. Store shelves have become battlegrounds.

Share

More and more, companies are engaging in share wars to boost volume and profit. If you can't attract new customers, you try to attract other people's customers. Minimally, you want to protect your share of your category from others; optimally, you want everybody else's share to be your own.

Share is significant for another less visible but important reason. It is one of the primary factors the investment community looks at in determining the health of a brand and its parent company. Anything with a strong impact on stock price is important because stock price affects bonuses, employment, stock options, and daily life in the office.

Ramifications

If a company doesn't perform to analysts' expectations, stock price drops, capitalization goes down, and less money is available for investment and growth.

So when a salesperson came to me with a product or service or when one of my co-workers was trying to sell an idea that would require investment, my concern was whether doing what was proposed would help me "make my numbers." I was a loyal employee and worked diligently so that my company would get ahead. I was also self-motivated.

When a company makes its numbers, more money is available to pay its employees bonuses. Bonuses are a big deal. Bonuses run anywhere from one percent of base salary to multiples of salaries such as 2x or 3x. The higher the title someone holds, the higher the bonus potential. As you can imagine, the dollar value of these bonuses is high, and the motivational power even higher.

Another motivational tool a company uses to encourage its employees to meet goals is the issuance of stock options. Stock options provided to management level employees entitle them to purchase shares at a pre-determined strike price. If the price of the stock goes up, the value of these options go up. In the case of companies like Microsoft, just a few options were worth millions of dollars. These provide additional motivation — and are extremely effective — at least until the employee becomes a multimillionaire and decides to retire.

One of the most powerful reasons that an employee wishes to make his numbers is that work life is much better when business is going well. When business is good, layoffs are rare and people feel secure in their jobs. Risks can be taken and new ideas pursued. Money is available for investment either in advertising, capital or personnel, which in turn spurs more growth. Happy company management pays attention to benefits, employee morale and other "softer" concerns.

When business is bad, you can be assured that management is not paying attention to "softer" concerns. They are intensely concentrating on how to deliver the number they promised their board of directors or privately held owner. There are nasty financial and emotional ramifications when numbers are missed.

When times are bad, attention paid by management goes up. Micromanaging becomes more common. Days, hours, weeks, and months are spent explaining why volume is bad. Re-planning becomes a way of life. Shipments are reviewed on an hourly basis. More data is reviewed. More presentations are written and given. More meetings are held to figure out what to do. Time that could have been spent on generating new ideas and growing the business is spent instead on defending it. It is a vicious cycle that is hard to escape.

Empathize

To understand your customers, you must think like they do. Step into their shoes and realize they are concerned with many of the same things as you: volume, profit, and share. In addition, time (or lack of it) is more of a factor in everything today. We read about how productivity has gone up drastically in recent history. Productivity has risen in part because of superior technology.

I can't remember how I worked without a personal computer. When I got out of graduate school and entered the work world, no one had such a thing. I remember coveting my secretary's (they weren't yet administrators) electric typewriter that had built-in white tape for erasures. We had no voice mail. No Internet or e-mail. Can you remember carbon paper? I can. Access to copying machines was limited. It has only been in the last three years that I realized I couldn't live without a cell phone.

Employees have more and more communication tools at their disposal. We can all be reached twenty-four hours a day, and often are. As company layoffs increase, each remaining employee takes on more and more responsibility. Juggling priorities is tough. But Priority One is always to make your numbers. This is easier said than done, however. Just concentrating on volume, merely wanting profit, pretending your share is up — none of these work. It takes time, effort, and the right strategies to move business forward.

When I was in the chair opposite you, when I was the buyer and you were the seller, I cared more about my business — not yours. Sometimes, although I knew you were trying to help me, I felt I had no time to listen.

You might ask a prospective customer for a meeting and state, "*All* I want is one hour of your time; that's it." And to yourself you're thinking that an hour is little to ask. After all, you're likely traveling from another state, or at least fighting traffic for substantially more than the hour you'd like your customer to listen.

I just want you to be aware of what that hour really means. Or, should I say, multiple hours. Since your customer is in the position to buy something from you, it is safe to assume that he or she is also in the position to buy something from others. Your customer interacts with multiple vendors, suppliers, and partners. Not just you.

When I was a customer, I received at least five cold-call voice mails a day. Some of these voice mails were surprisingly long. After three minutes of message, I would delete the voice mail whether finished or not, so assume only fifteen minutes listening to potential supplier messages per day. Some customers will receive more calls, some less; but all receive unsolicited calls.

In addition, I also had consistent contact with supplier partners that I was already buying from. Sometimes this contact was in conjunction with a project. Sometimes this contact was initiated by the salesperson's desire to maintain open communication (and future sales) with me. Given that I worked with many different groups, I would estimate that I spoke to current partners on average two to three times a day for an average of fifteen minutes each. That's 45 minutes staying current with those who are helping me.

Finally, I did spare hours to people who had services or goods that intrigued me, particularly those who knew what motivated me, as I hope you will after reading this chapter. On average, I would meet with outside suppliers for one hour per day. These meetings weren't always one hour or always one per day. But five, hour-long meetings each week would not be unusual.

So, add up all the time spent talking to salespersons: 15 minutes + 45 minutes + 60 minutes = 120 minutes = 2 hours per day = 10 hours per week. One full workday was spent talking with suppliers. As a customer, it's seldom about the time required for one meeting. It's the time needed in aggregate.

We all desire to spend our time more wisely, if not doing the right things, at least in spending time with people we like. Which brings me to the next thing you should know. Relationships matter. I would work with someone I didn't care for, but I didn't enjoy it. I would not work with someone I didn't trust; at least not if I had control over the situation.

When you work with someone over a period of time, projects become easier. Your contact knows what you like and need. Connections with related departments are established. Uncertainty is reduced because if they performed well in the past, it is likely they will do so in the future. Finally, in some cases, you genuinely care for the person you're working with. You become friendly beyond your supplier-buyer relationship.

Some companies today are leery of this. To ensure that relationships will not impede business decisions, employees are forbidden from accepting gifts or meals from outside suppliers. Without interaction, it is more difficult to form relationships. Companies do not want even the appearance of business being "bought."

With all things equal, I would rather work with someone I like and respect. Everybody would. But don't let these seemingly airtight relationships lead you astray. A friend of mine was charged with the task of telling a beloved, reliable, long-term supplier that her company was moving all their business to a competitor. My friend said she left the boardroom after giving them the news and cried. She said it was one of the hardest tasks she'd ever done. But she did it. When push came to shove, the decision was not made because of relationship. It was made because hundreds of thousands of dollars would be saved as a result of the change. Ultimately it was because of profit.

Advice

To understand your customer, you need know only this: Your customer wants to make his numbers. He wants to sell more. He wants to make more money. He wants to beat his competition. He wants to work with someone he likes and trusts, and he'd prefer that you spend your time (instead of his spending his time) ensuring things happen.

If you are making a preliminary sales call, try to learn what motivates your prospect the most: volume, profit, or share. The importance of volume in comparison to profit or share varies for each business. During the heyday of dot-coms in the late 1990's, new companies focused on volume and share. Profit was less important (and profit was rare — which foreshadowed the eventual death of many of these new companies). A company with strong competition and already high volume, such as Coca-Cola, will focus on share — constantly monitoring (and working to get) Pepsi Cola volume.

If you are able to determine whether your customer is most interested in volume, profit, or share, you will present the right products and selling stories. If you tie your product, idea, or service to the end result — how it will impact volume, profit, or share — you will be sure to gain the customer's attention.

When volume is most desired, customers will buy products or services that help them move volume. If profit is the key, budgets will be tight and all purchases viewed against whether or not they will eventually bring in a positive return. If you can help a company vis-á-vis its competitor when share is a priority, you are in a good spot.

If you cannot determine which is the most important objective for your prospect, tie your product or service back to all three. Emphasize profit above all. Companies are in business to make money. The dot-com companies who ignored profit (and their shareholders) have learned this the hard way.

Customer Priority	Selling Strategy
Volume	Ties to increased sales. Quantify how volume will increase if purchase is made.
Profit	Tie to increased profit. Focus on money to be saved or additional revenues that can be generated.
Share	Tie to how an advantage will be created versus competition. Illustrate the benefits for their company and pitfalls for others.

It's all about looking at things from your potential customer's point-of-view. It is about avoiding the trap of looking at things from your own reference point. Sure, your job is hard, you have numbers to make as well, but in the long run if you think like the customer that you are trying to sell to, you will make more sales and help everyone grow.

The better your customers do, the more they will have to spend with you in the future.

About Sara Owens

Sara Owens is founder and President of Promo Pros, Inc., a Promotion consulting firm based in St. Louis, Missouri. Promo Pros, Inc. is focused on consumer promotion optimization — from development through execution through analysis. With nearly two decades of experience in marketing and marketing services, Sara knows what it's like to be a consumer packaged goods marketer. If you work for a marketing company, or sell to a marketing company, Sara can help you understand how consumer promotion programs affect overall objectives of increasing volume, generating profit and gaining share. On-the-job experience comes from the two largest food companies in the U.S. — Sara built and ran ConAgra Frozen Foods' Marketing Development and Consumer Promotions department and worked for Kraft Foods in the areas of packaging, marketing, and consumer promotions. In addition to her solid consumer packaged goods experience, Sara has financial services experience from Household International. Having worked five years on the agency side — in both advertising and promotion — she knows what it's like to be on "both sides of the wall." Sara received her Bachelors degree in Communications and her Masters degree in Advertising from Northwestern University in Evanston, Illinois.

Contact Information:
Sara Owens
Promo Pros, Inc.
St. Louis, MO
Phone: (314) 322-6645
Fax: (314) 989-1565
E-mail: sara@promo-pros.com
Website: www.promo-pros.com

CONVICTABLE COMMITMENT
The Key to Achieving Your Goals

by Andre L. Beaudoin

If you were accused of being committed to your goals would there be sufficient evidence to convict you?

The Fallacy of Goal Setting

Setting goals is touted by many of the world's great sales gurus as the key to success in sales and in life itself. *It isn't.* Every day hundreds — perhaps thousands — of sales people set goals. They write them down and set dates for their achievement, but often fail to attain them. Each year millions — perhaps billions — of people set goals designed to change their lives for the better. On January 1, year after year, individuals make New Year's resolutions that most forget by month's end.

Committing to your goals, not setting them, is the secret to success. The degree to which you are honestly willing to do whatever it takes to reach your objectives determines the potential you have to succeed. Your personal beliefs, attitudes, values, and the support you receive from outside sources all affect your ability to establish and maintain a high commitment level. Maintaining a balanced personal life and appropriate focus on desired outcomes will insure that you have the energy and support necessary to overcome the obstacles you encounter while pursuing your goals.

Commitment Level

The degree to which you are committed to your goals is directly proportional to the level of success you will have in achieving them. If you have written your goals down but can't remember what they are or where you put the paper they were written on, there is virtually no chance you will accomplish them. If, on the other hand, you have written them down, set dates for their accomplishment, review them daily, share them with others, have a plan for achieving them, work the plan, and believe they are achievable, you just might have convictable commitment, and your likelihood of attaining your goals is many times greater.

By now you are probably thinking, "What is a convictable commitment?" Fair enough; let's define it. The dictionary defines commitment as "a strong dedication." To be convicted means "to be proven guilty in a court of law." For a conviction to take place there needs to be sufficient evidence, witnesses, and proof of actions taken to demonstrate beyond doubt that the accusation made is truthful. A convictable commitment, then, is a strong dedication that can be proven through the use of evidence, witnesses, and demonstrated actions. The best example I have of the miraculous, unstoppable power of this level of commitment was provided to me by Armand and Florence, a couple I had the honor of knowing as I grew up.

In August of 1957 Armand and Florence were celebrating on a beach in Bridgeport, Connecticut. They were clapping, cheering, and jumping up and down while taking pictures of their son, who had just taken his very first steps. If you are a parent, grandparent, aunt, uncle, or friend of a parent whose child has just begun walking, you know how excited they were. Three days later they were standing in a hospital corridor, looking through a plate glass window into a critical care unit. Their fifteen-month-old child was lying motionless on a bed next to an iron lung.

A doctor came into the corridor to explain their son's condition. "Your child has contracted polio. He has lost all motor functions. It's likely that he will soon be unable to breathe on his own. We may need the iron lung. Your son will never move. He will never have the strength to raise his head off his pillow. I recommend that you commit him to a permanent care facility."

As Florence began to cry and tremble with emotion, Armand put his arms around his wife and made a convictable commitment. "We will bring our son home. He will have a family and a life with human dignity." Then this couple took the actions that could convict them of their commitment. Armand took on a second full-time job to support his family and meet the rapidly mounting medical bills. Florence reported to the hospital each and every day, seven days a week, learning to provide the massages and physical therapy necessary to keep her son alive. Armand and Florence maintained these activities for days, then weeks, then months, despite the lack of change in their son's condition.

Finally, on a cold, wet, typical New England winter day, Florence entered her son's hospital room. As she stretched out her hand to begin a massage, he lifted his shoulder from the bed for the first time. This was the first reward Armand and Florence received for maintaining their commitment. With the belief that continued effort would result in additional gain, they maintained this level of commitment for twelve more years. Armand worked two jobs, and Florence provided four to six hours per day of physical therapy. They went on to fight the battles with schools and service agencies necessary to insure their son's full participation in life. Today he lives in his own home with his wife and two daughters. He travels independently with the aid of crutches and a wheelchair, and he enjoys a life with human dignity.

That's a convictable commitment . . . evidenced in writing by reams of letters and medical forms; witnessed by the doctors, nurses, relatives, and friends who aided in their son's recovery; and demonstrated by the actions that transformed a stricken boy from human vegetable to human being. It is a convictable commitment I witnessed personally. Armand and Florence are my parents, and I am the child who doctors believed would "never have the strength to raise his head off his pillow."

How does your commitment level measure up?

0——1——2——3——4——5——6——7——8——9——10
Innocent   Convictable

What are your goals? Are they written down? Is there a piece of paper, a floppy disk, or a hard drive that could be submitted into court as evidence of your goals? Have you shared your goals with your family, friends, and associates? Are there witnesses who could be called to the stand to testify that you have stated your goals and your plans to achieve them? If your actions were observed for an entire day, would they demonstrate beyond a shadow of a doubt that you are working towards your goals? If you were accused of being committed to your goals, would there be sufficient evidence to convict you?

Maintaining a Balanced Life

Balanced goals are the secret to establishing and maintaining the energy level necessary to support a convictable commitment. The myopic focus of all your energy on a single goal may result in its achievement, but the price paid will always exceed the value received. Winning this year's "Salesman of the Year" award can't substitute for the feelings of pride experienced by attending your child's first play or concert. A moment of fame, a large commission check, and the one-time accolades of your associates can't replace the life-long pleasures of friends and family, good health, or a strong spiritual connection with God, nature, or the higher power of your choice. Unless a careful balance of career, family, health, educational, social, and spiritual aspects of life are maintained, the achievement of a single objective will be a hollow victory.

Answering the Reverend Robert Schuller's question, "What would you do if you knew you could not fail?" for each aspect of life is a great way to begin the process of balancing your life. Answer each of the following questions, and use these answers to develop a meaningful goal for each aspect of your life.

- What do I want to accomplish or change to improve my career?

- What would I do for my family if I had unlimited time and resources?

- How can I improve or maintain my current physical condition?

- What do I need to know or learn to insure my continued growth and understanding of the world I live in?

- Whom would I choose as friends, and how would I socialize with them if I weren't influenced by the opinions of others?

- What are my spiritual beliefs and how do I demonstrate them?

Answering these questions will reveal your personal beliefs, attitudes, and values. Choose one objective to focus on for each of these aspects. Write these down to create evidence of your goals. Share each objective with three to five people who will be directly affected as you progress toward it, and you'll have witnesses who can be called to testify about your goals. Create a step-by-step plan for achieving each goal and implement these plans to demonstrate your commitment.

Benefits of Balance

Maintaining a balanced life has an additional obvious but often overlooked benefit for sales people. I refer to it as "natural networking." Providing increased support from family and friends, this process is a powerful advantage for the professional sales person. During the inevitable slumps and slow times, or when increased time and effort are needed to close a "big" deal, the support of family and friends can be critical.

Networking has become a recognized part of most companies' marketing mix. Natural networking is the result of relationships that build when you are pursuing your social, health, education, or spiritual goals. Good networkers know that it is relationship building, not attending weekly or monthly meetings, that results in quality referrals and new business.

Actively participating in a club related to one of your hobbies, frequenting a gym, taking an adult education course, or attending church services will likely introduce you to people you wouldn't meet on the job or at a networking function. The defensive posture taken by network function attendees trying to sell while protecting themselves from being sold doesn't exist in these other venues. Strong personal relationships can be built, founded on the common ground of the hobby, activity, topic, or beliefs you have in common with the other members of these groups. Discussions of the services you provide related to your career become a natural part of conversation and don't require a snappy, well-rehearsed introduction or elevator pitch. Referrals from these friends to their friends provide a higher initial trust factor than any other type of lead. Best of all, you are doing something you enjoy while these relationships are building.

The support of your spouse, children, parents, or siblings can have an incredible impact on your energy level and attitude. When your family knows that you have set aside time for them, they will be much more understanding when you need a shoulder to lean on or to spend extra time addressing a particularly difficult situation.

The husband or wife who knows you care is more likely to have a dinner plate in the microwave when you come home late than to meet you at the door with cutting remarks about how inconsiderate you are. The parent who receives a phone call or visit once a week is more likely to brag to his or her friends about the great job you have than to complain about how your career leaves you no time to say hello.

Consider the effect the above scenarios could have on your attitude and energy. Wouldn't you feel better about yourself if your parents were bragging about you rather than criticizing you? Wouldn't you prefer to be supported when things are tough rather than blamed? Your focus on your family's needs determines their focus on yours. Love is the most powerful force in the universe and it's inexhaustible. The more you give the more you'll receive. Give yours generously and you'll be supercharged.

Maintaining Focus

Unlike our desktop, laptop, and handheld computers, few of us mere mortals are capable of maintaining the level of multitasking that modern life demands. Concentrating on more than one thing at a time often results in poor performance on all fronts. How often have you forgotten to pick up the bread or the dry cleaning on the way home because you were thinking about an over-stimulating day at the office? Given our propensity to forget and the stimulus overload we face on most days, how, you wonder, can you simultaneously focus on six goals, each associated with a different aspect of life?

Paradoxically, the answer is *don't concentrate* on the goals.

Concentrating is a conscious activity, and our conscious minds are not designed to handle multiple complex tasks in an optimal manner. If you had to depend on your conscious mind for ordinary bodily functions like breathing, blinking, or pumping blood through your body, how long do you think you would last? Have someone toss you a ball. (I suggest a nerf ball for this exercise to insure no one gets hurt.) Rather than allowing your body to automatically catch it, try to do it consciously. Concentrate on exactly how much effort you should use to lift your arm, open your hand, focus your eyes, and coordinate the many other actions you need to do this simple task successfully.

Concentrating or focusing on multiple goals is just as confusing as trying to consciously catch the ball. Moreover, this fragmented thinking can be depressing and damaging to your self-esteem and attitude. If you are constantly focused on where you want to go or what you want to be, you are subconsciously telling yourself that you are not good enough in the here and now. If you are focused on all the things you need to do to reach your objectives, the sheer volume of work ahead of you will be overwhelming.

Instead, why not use the same subconscious mental powers to achieve your goals that you so fluently use to manage all the complex aspects of your body's functioning. You have grown from an infant to an adult without consciously focusing on everything that needed to be done. Once you have learned the basic skills, your mind and body take you through many complex daily tasks — bicycling, driving, reading — without conscious thought of every detailed action required for these routines. Consider the possibility that progressing from where you are in your sales career to where you want to be can be done the same way. For that matter, why shouldn't this system apply to achieving the goals in each aspect of your life?

This is not to say that you can succeed without some conscious thought and effort. Maturing from infancy to adulthood did require conscious effort to eat and study, for instance. Learning to read required mastery of the mechanics of phonics, word meaning, and sentence structure. So, too, focusing effectively on your goals — whether they are related to sales or personal growth — requires mastery of a simple, conscious technique to focus your subconscious mind on achieving your desired objectives. The solution is to use "affirmations."

Affirmations are simple, positive, present-tense statements that put your visions into words. Effective affirmations have two parts, the primary statement followed by a defining phrase. They express ideas as realities.

Example: I am healthy, providing myself the rest, nutrition, and exercise necessary to maintain my physical and mental well being.

"I am healthy" is the primary statement: simple, positive, present tense. The balance of the affirmation is the defining phrase. This element serves as a reminder of the actions necessary to realize the primary statement.

Affirmations work by programming into your subconscious mind the reality you wish to achieve. By repeating your affirmations daily, you focus your powerful subconscious mind on the task of manifesting your desires. The tricky part of mastering this technique is learning to go with the flow and consciously take the actions your subconscious suggests. As an infant, you accepted the food your parents fed you. As a sales trainee, you accepted the theories you were taught. To successfully use affirmations, you must be willing to become more intuitive — paying attention to and acting on your instincts — and less intellectual, trying to consciously figure everything out.

Using the Convictable Commitment System

The Think/Write and Convictable Commitment worksheets included at the end of this chapter can be used to develop your commitment to a convictable level.

Step 1

Set aside an hour or two to sit quietly and fill in the Think/Write sheet. Get comfortable. Take a few long, deep breaths. Close your eyes and think about what you would like to achieve in a single aspect of your life. Use the questions in the Balance section of this chapter to get started. Let your mind drift, and think of as many goals and objectives as you can for this first aspect. Then enter them on the Think/Write sheet beside that heading. Repeat this process for each of the six aspects of life. Think first, for ten or more minutes, then write. (The act of writing creates a focus that can interfere with the thinking process and limit the number of ideas that will come to mind.)

Step 2

Review what you have written and choose the one goal you would most like to achieve for each of the six aspects of life.

Specify dates for each objective to be achieved. Write each goal and its date in the appropriate box in the Evidence column of the Convictable Commitment Worksheet.

Step 3

Choose three to five people to act as witnesses. Witnesses should be people who have a vested interest in your reaching your objective. Family members make good witnesses for family goals, bosses and associates for career goals, doctors for health goals. Write the witnesses' names in the appropriate boxes on the worksheet.

Step 4

Devise a plan of action for achieving your goal. If your goal will require more than 90 days to achieve, break it down into steps that can be reached in a shorter period. Long-term goals are commendable, but are seldom achieved if not broken down into multiple short-term goals that can be achieved and celebrated along the way. Outline your 90-day plan of action in the appropriate box on the Convictable Commitment Worksheet.

Step 5

In the last column of the worksheet, write your goals as affirmations. Very simply state each goal as a positive, present-tense statement with a reminder of how you are going to achieve it. For example, if your goal is to increase your personal sales and your plan includes more prospecting and improved sales skills, your affirmation might be: "I am selling more than ever before, prospecting harder, listening better, and presenting solutions my clients desire."

Step 6

Put your ego on the line. Within 48 hours of completing the worksheet, contact all of your witnesses and share your goals and plans with them. If you really want to demonstrate convictable commitment, arrange a weekly or monthly meeting with them to review your progress.

Step 7

Read your affirmations aloud three times daily and implement your plans.

When you take these steps, there will be sufficient evidence to convict you of your goals, and you will experience the rewards of Convictable Commitment.

Think — Write

Profession: _____

_____

_____

Family: _____

_____

_____

Education: _____

_____

_____

Health: _____

_____

_____

Social: _____

_____

_____

Spiritual: _____

_____

_____

Convictable Commitment Worksheet

Aspect Definition:	Evidence Written, dated goal	Witnesses 3-5 people told	Action(s) What is being done	Affirmation Verbalized vision
Profession				
Family				
Education				
Health				
Social				
Spiritual				

©2002 Andre L. Beaudoin

About Andre L. Beaudoin

*A*ndre L. Beaudoin is a professional speaker who inspires and teaches organizations and individuals to achieve more. When he was totally paralyzed by polio at fifteen months old, Andre's parents were told he would never have the strength to raise his head off his pillow. From this inauspicious beginning, Andre has achieved respect and recognition as a successful salesman, sales manager, businessman, entrepreneur, and father. While earning his marketing degree, Andre sold and managed sales teams for the Fuller Brush Co. and Cutco Cutlery. During his tenure with Homecraft Industries, he expanded a local phone room with 18 employees into a regional telemarketing center with four offices employing over 300 sales people. He founded ProActive Marketing in 1990, a telemarketing services company, and in 1999 Andre Inspires, his inspirational speaking and consulting business. Andre's professional sales and training experience combined with his provocative model of goal setting and accomplishment increases the commitment and performance of individuals and the organizations they work for to levels they never dreamed possible.

Contact Information:
Andre L. Beaudoin
Andre Inspires
38 Country Lane
Meriden CT 06451-2711
Phone: (800) 205-6958
Fax: 800-856-4250
E-mail: andre@andreinspires.com
Website: www.andreinspires.com

The Winning Mindset in Sales

by Dr. Bill Newman

Growing up on a dairy farm, the youngest of nine children and weighing 125 pounds by fourth grade, was not easy for Rulon Gardner. The kids teased him about his shape and called him "Fatso." His childhood "was kind of tough," he told reporters, because of the teasing. But he rose above it. "I used those insults as motivation," he said. That motivation got him in the improbable situation of facing Alexander Karelin, winner of three Olympic gold medals and widely acknowledged as the greatest Greco-Roman wrestler of all time. Karelin, a Russian, had never lost in international competition and had not conceded a point in ten years. But that was before he met Gardner, an American from Wyoming, at the 2000 Sydney Olympics.

It was a match no one thought Rulon Gardner could win. "I'm not as strong as him, not even close," Garner later said. "I knew if I let him push me around, get even two or three points on me, it was over."

Karelin, whose throwing skills are so renowned that he has a lift named for him, tried to throw Gardner around in the first two minutes but could not. Gardner stayed chest-to-chest, shoulder-to-shoulder, never letting Karelin get leverage or a chance to score points by tossing him.

The key moment came after the first scoreless three minutes. At that point, the wrestlers began the second period with a clinch and had to remain locked until one executed a scoring move or released his lock. As they powered each other to the side of the mat, Gardner managed to keep his hands clinched, but Karelin's slipped apart. Gardner received a point and won. They called it "The Miracle of the Mat."

When questioned by the press, Gardner replied, "When did I think I could beat him? About ten minutes ago. I kept saying 'I think I can. I think I can.' But it wasn't until it was over that I knew I could."

Rulon Gardner's winning mindset so strongly dominated his thinking that he made history. He came a long way from the negative self-image of "Fatso" to a positive self-image as a gold-medal-winning athlete. His positive, present thoughts about himself directed him to a vision of the future that propelled him to become what he imagined he could be. His winning mindset moved him to winning the Olympic super heavyweight wrestling gold medal!

A winning mindset toward sales is rooted in a winning mindset toward life. The moment-by-moment choices we make about our thoughts and actions, both intrapersonally and interpersonally, directly impact the successful result or outcome of our experiences. We condition our minds to expect to win.

Some people believe that winning means at the expense of others, that if one of us wins the other loses. To presuppose that, for someone to win someone else has to lose, means it's either you or me. That works on the sports field. But in sales, as in other areas of life, when we shift our thinking to win/win, we realize we all can win, versus a worldview of win or lose. This attitudinal shift in our thinking to win/win is a highly conscious choice to value the idea of "you *and* me" over the former belief of "you *or* me." This is a transformational shift from a focus on "me" to a focus on "we."

This mental shift of a value choice is individually, corporately, and globally transformational. The belief that "the whole world loves a winner" evolves to "the whole world loves winning together."

Our choice to value a win/win alternative over a win/lose one is a choice to value what the other person wants or needs as much as what you want or need. When Jesus Christ was asked to choose the "greatest commandment," he stated, "Love the Lord your God with all your heart, mind, soul, and strength and your neighbor as yourself." A win/win choice is not unselfish but rather an enlightened self-interest that clearly understands and believes that the interests of others are equal to those of oneself. One lives life with the conviction that the playing field of sales, as in life, is played on a level field of equality at all times. One's business life as a salesperson is not mutually exclusive or oppositional to one's personal life. Rather, one's business life and personal life are synergistic. Our awareness and focus on our "being" precedes the success of our "doing" in our business life, as in our personal life.

A winning mindset in sales maintains a perspective that in the business of sales, as in life, relationships are the highest value. One's success both personally and professionally is created from winning relationships, which are the real bottom line. This requires a creative thinking process that breaks restrictive, selfish patterns of all or nothing, black or white, or attack or defend.

Instead of working harder to try to make everything work, it is a choice to work smarter by using our intuition and creativity to determine the greatest good for all involved. The choice to create a solution that is best for all is a solution for a win/win alternative over a win/lose experience. This choice of win/win creates harmony between ourselves and others, interpersonally, and within ourselves intrapersonally.

The mindset of a winner in sales begins with an open, honest, caring attitude about helping each customer obtain what he or she really wants and needs. As a win/win salesperson, you will empathetically feel and sympathetically care for your customer as you would want him to look out for your interests when you are his customer. This winning mindset of integrity is the creative origin of the harmonious relationship between a successful salesperson and her or his customers.

A winner in sales very simply understands that customers want their needs met. Therefore, a winner in sales gives customers the opportunity to purchase products and services with complete integrity in the relationship. The focus is always on the customer rather than on the salesperson or on the product or service. The art of persuasion or manipulation is absent from their win/win relationships. The egalitarian nature of the mindset of a winner in sales simultaneously frees the customer and salesperson both to experience a sense of victory.

Smart sales people build quality relationships with their customers. They see the ultimate purpose of every sale is to create and nurture customer relationships. Just as bad relationships lead to bad business, better relationships lead to better business. The mindset of a winner in sales focuses on how the product or service of the salesperson is going to provide a solution to the needs of their customers. Customers buy the solutions that your products or services deliver to meet their needs and reinforce their values.

The sincere focus on and interest in the customer enable the salesperson to establish an environment in which the customer feels secure enough to disclose his/her needs and values. To establish such rapport with your customers, you must first know what you most value, need and want in the relationship with each unique customer or client who presents you with a selling opportunity. You cannot facilitate rapport with effective questioning about what your customer or client values, needs, and wants until you begin with yourself.

The winning mindset of sales requires transformation that turns win/lose problems into win/win solutions. Your role as a transformation agent in sales parallels the role of a winning executive coach. My good friend and colleague, Steve Lishansky, CEO of Success Dynamics in Concord, MA, teaches the students of his Executive Coaching Institute, "Your job is to facilitate what is most important to the client, and to add value to the client and his or her organization."

Lishansky adds, "If you want lasting, meaningful transformation that continues to grow over time, you need to address the source of transformation as well as results. This must include a shift of what we call the mindset. This shift of the mindset is the foundation for creating profound and lasting transformation, different actions, as well as a significant improvement in results. The equation below is our formula for producing transformation and results (inspired by and adapted from the outstanding work of Chris Argyres.)

$$\text{Mindset} + \text{Action} = \text{Result}"$$

Steve teaches his students a "Framework for Transformation" wherein he states: "The reasons we focus primarily on shifting the observer are:

1. Transformation of the being (the observer) will produce profound changes in the action.

2. To produce long-lasting transformation you must transform the being (changing the action does not usually produce lasting transformation).

3. The actions and choice of actions change organically when the being changes because how you see the world determines how you will act in it.

4. How we see the world is primarily a function of our beliefs and subconscious, habitual, neurological 'wiring.'

5. Habits, driven by emotionally embedded intensity, which are often rules and beliefs, determine what filters are triggered among the VtR elements (identity, values, beliefs, rules, incantations, vehicles etc.).

6. Connection to a high level of being comes from the alignment of identity, purpose, and values.

7. High-level transformation takes place in the movement from lower levels of VtR (i.e. rules and beliefs, strategies and tactics, to higher levels (i.e. values and identity, vision and mission)."

The references that Steve Lishansky makes above to VtR refer to another program he teaches called "Vision to Reality." Please refer to the chart, "Clarifying Your Life Vision, From Kaleidoscope to Telescope," for a powerful depiction of the conscious and subconscious elements of the dynamics of human thought and behavior.

This chart illustrates ways for shifting the observer and explains more explicitly the origin of the development of a winning mindset in sales.

Clarifying Your Life Vision
From Kaleidoscope to Telescope
The Keys to Fulfillment — The Telescope of Life

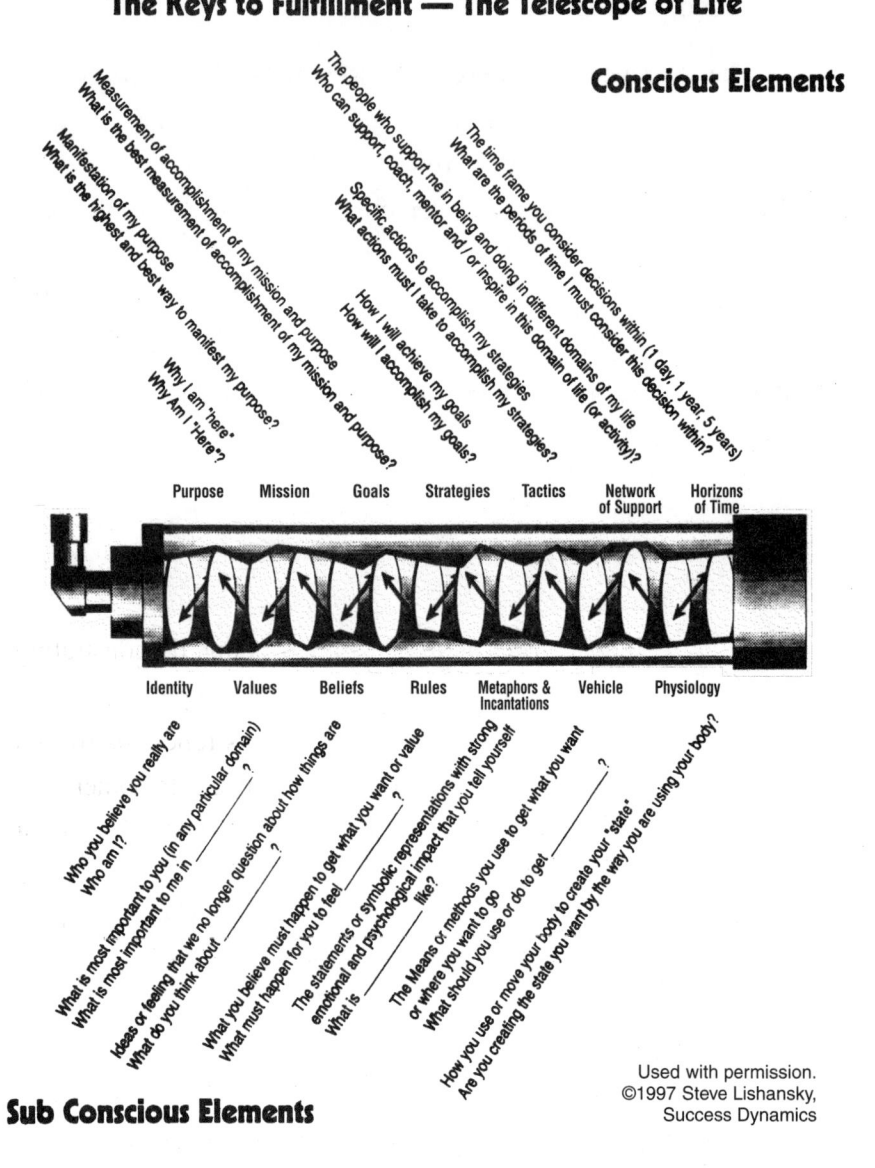

Conscious Elements

- Manifestation of my purpose / What is the highest and best way to manifest my purpose?
- Measurement of accomplishment of my mission and purpose / What is the best measurement of accomplishment of my mission and purpose?
- Why I am "here" / Why Am I "Here"?
- The people who support me in being and doing in different domains of my life / Who can support, coach, mentor and/or inspire in this domain of life (or activity)?
- Specific actions to accomplish my strategies / What actions must I take to accomplish my strategies?
- How I will achieve my goals / How will I accomplish my goals?
- The time frame you consider decisions within (1 day, 1 year, 5 years) / What are the periods of time I must consider this decision within?

Purpose | Mission | Goals | Strategies | Tactics | Network of Support | Horizons of Time

Identity | Values | Beliefs | Rules | Metaphors & Incantations | Vehicle | Physiology

- Who you believe you really are / Who am I?
- What is most important to you (in any particular domain) / What is most important to me in _____?
- Ideas or feeling that we no longer question about how things are / What do you think about _____?
- What you believe must happen to get what you want or value / What must happen for you to feel _____?
- The statements or symbolic representations with strong emotional and psychological impact that you tell yourself / What is _____ like?
- The Means or methods you use to get what you want / Where you want to go or what should you use or do to get _____?
- How you use or move your body to create your "state" / Are you creating the state you want by the way you are using your body?

Sub Conscious Elements

Used with permission.
©1997 Steve Lishansky,
Success Dynamics

High-level transformation is heartwarmingly told in the story of the musical *Annie*. The story revolves around the heartless billionaire, Daddy Warbucks, who owns much materially but enjoys no love in his life. His transformation begins when he invites an orphan, Annie, to spend Christmas with him, as a public relations gesture.

As is natural for children, Annie innocently and freely lives without pretensions. Or more specifically, as a spiritual being of love having a human experience. Annie's identity and purpose were subconsciously and automatically reflected in what mattered to her most, her value of love. Annie's loving presence and "being" creates a defining moment and transformational catalyst for Daddy Warbucks.

Prior to her visit, he had lived his miserable life at a level of "doing" which included strategies, rules and tactics for becoming materially wealthier. However, Annie's stay melts his heart and teaches him that love is the highest and most important value in life.

Annie automatically functions from her being, demonstrating the most important value in her life is love, and the purpose of her life is to give love. In contrast, Daddy Warbucks functions from a place of doing for wealth, with little care or concern for others.

Before Annie teaches Daddy Warbucks that he must treat people with respect, care and love, Daddy Warbucks says, "I never saw any reason to be nice to the people on the way up, because I have no intention of going back down." This line always gets a round of applause because the audience can identify with it so much from their life experiences with people who hold beliefs similar to Daddy Warbucks'.

The impact of Orphan Annie on Daddy Warbucks produced a shift in his mindset from win/lose to win/win. His transformation occurred when he moved from lower levels of rules and beliefs and strategies and tactics about wealth accumulation without concern for others to higher levels of identity, purpose, values, mission and vision.

When Daddy Warbucks shifted his highest value from wealth accumulation, without care for others, to love and care for others, he also shifted his belief and rules about how to treat other people.

The clearer your understanding of your own identity, purpose, values, mission, and vision, the easier it will be to reach your full potential as the salesperson you are capable of becoming because you will cultivate and inspire the greatness within you!

Think of Rulon Gardner. Mindshift is a complex and powerful thing. In a tense moment, a moment he prepared for years, he simplified the process and tapped into his power by telling himself, "I think I can." When you have your mind set for win/win interactions with your customers, you will tap your greatest selling power which flows directly from your "being" before the success of your "doing." You will also open the door to your unique selling proposition.

Your unique selling proposition is derived from your insight about the following questions. What is it about you that makes you unique? What makes you different from others in sales? Are you transformable? Do you conscientiously strive to build win/win relationships? As a package, these are the essence of a winning mindset in sales.

It helps to remember that the winning mindset of sales is the same as the winning mindset of life. Our success in sales, as our success in life, is directly related to how we think about ourselves and others. This is a universal wisdom observed through the ages. Epictitus said, "Men are not disturbed by things, but by the view which they take of things." Roman Emperor Marcus Aurelius stated, "Our life is what our thoughts make it." William Shakespeare wrote in *Hamlet*, "Nothing in the world is good or bad, but thinking makes it so." And Emerson observed with compelling simplicity, "Life consists in what a man is thinking all day."

From ancient times to the present, the sustainable truth has been that we are as we think about ourselves in the past and present, and we become as we think about ourselves in the future. The good news is, this means that we actually create our identity, purpose, mission and vision by how we choose to think about ourselves and what we choose to value. If we choose to think about ourselves in the present with high self-esteem and imagine our future in congruence with our present thoughts and beliefs about our high self-esteem, we will achieve the successful objectives we imagine. This vision of the future starts with our thoughts about ourselves in the present which leads to the reality in our futures.

In his book, *The Six Pillars Of Self-Esteem*, psychologist Nathaniel Branden describes self-esteem as follows, "Self-esteem, fully realized, is our ability to cope with the basic challenges of life; and confidence in our right to be successful and happy, the feeling of being worthy, deserving, entitled to assert our needs and wants, achieve our values, and enjoy the fruits of our efforts. To trust one's mind and to know that one is worthy of happiness is the essence of self-esteem. The power of this conviction about oneself lies in the fact that it is more than a judgment or feeling. It is a motivator. It inspires behavior. In turn, it is directly affected by how we act. Causation flows in both directions. There is a continuous feedback loop between our actions in the world and our self-esteem. The level of our self-esteem influences how we act, and how we act influences the level of our self-esteem."

An obstacle to the winning mindset for sales and life is when our conscious, positive thoughts and beliefs about ourselves are in discrepancy with our unconscious negative thoughts and beliefs. This unconscious discrepancy becomes conscious when we experience problems of maladjustment in life. These problems occur when we are not able to integrate our reactions to events with our positive, conscious belief about our self or our self-image. You feel bad about yourself because there is a dissonance between your self-image and your reaction to your experience.

Dr. Sigmund Freud studied the subconscious mind and the dynamic effect of dysfunctional thinking that can come from it. Psychologist Carl Rogers found that all people form images of themselves in their subconscious minds. That self-image sets the limit of each person's psychological development. A person cannot grow beyond the self-image of his or her subconscious mind. Our self-image may be an obstacle to our winning mindset because, if it is low, weak or negative, it puts a limit on what we can accomplish or achieve. However, if we change our negative self-image by identifying and stopping our negative, false, and limiting thoughts, beliefs, and rules about ourselves, we can positively expand our self-image to fulfill our potential for a winning mindset in sales.

Andrew Carnegie, a high school dropout, arrived from

Scotland penniless. He worked as a telegraph operator for the Pennsylvania Railroad for twelve years. He did not allow his lack of education to lead to a negative and low self-image. Rather he chose to see himself with a high self-image and to think of himself with confidence and competence in the present with a vision of personal and business success in the future.

Andrew Carnegie became the richest man in the world because he saw the potential of steel beams for railway-bridge construction, rather than wood trestles. His simple insight was the spark that started the Carnegie Steel Company, which he later sold to U.S. Steel in 1901 for the astronomical sum of $250 million.

Andrew Carnegie wanted to give the world his secrets of success. Lacking the education to write a book, he hired Napoleon Hill, a newspaper editor and later a speech writer for President Franklin Delano Roosevelt. Hill penned the famous statement, "Let me assert my firm belief that the only thing we have to fear is fear itself — nameless, unreasoning, unjustified terror which paralyzes needed efforts to convert retreat to advance." Hill probably developed the idea from Henry David Thoreau who wrote: "Nothing is so much to be feared as fear."

Napoleon Hill followed Andrew Carnegie around for many years, observing all that the billionaire did and said.. From this experience he wrote the book, *Think And Grow Rich*. It became the first great self-help book about self-image psychology.

Hill wrote in the book's preface, "In every chapter of this book, mention has been made of the money-making secret which has made fortunes for hundreds of exceedingly wealthy men whom I have carefully analyzed over a long period of years. The secret was brought to my attention by Andrew Carnegie. The canny lovable old Scotsman carelessly tossed it into my mind, when I was but a boy. Then he sat back in his chair, with a merry twinkle in his eyes, and watched carefully to see if I had brains enough to understand the full significance of what he had said to me. When he saw that I had grasped the idea, he asked if I would be willing to spend twenty years or more preparing myself to take it to the world, to men and women who, without the secret, might go through as failures. I said I would, and with Mr. Carnegie's cooperation, I have kept my promise."

During his time, Carnegie interacted with hundreds of self-made millionaires. As he developed relationships with all of them, he saw a common pattern among them. They shared a common denominator of knowing what they wanted and what it would be like to be successful. Mentally, they experienced their success long before they achieved it because they could create a visual image of their success. Hill called this ability to experience the future, "imagizing." This is what we now call visualizing the future or visioning. Your vision is based on your identity, purpose values, and mission directed to the future with a very clear visualization of your success in the future. The high achievers Carnegie knew were able to imagine or create in their mind, the experience of success before it happened. When Andrew Carnegie looked at the wooden trestle railroad bridge and visualized steel replacing the wood beams, he saw himself owning a great steel mill where steel sales people worked for him with a winning mindset in sales.

This winning mindset of Andrew Carnegie, as Hill wrote, requires that we change our subconscious thoughts by projecting into the subconscious the experience of great success. This is "imagizing" or visualizing yourself with high self-esteem and self-confidence and competence, achieving what is most important to you or what you value in your experience of great success in sales.

Your winning mindset in sales begins with clarity about your high, positive self-image of yourself that tells you who you are, your identity. You imagine what you would love clients to be saying about who you are and you then visualize it. You then clarify your values or what is most important to you in your sales relationships with your clients. You imagine what is most important to you about how you treat people and your clients and you visualize it. Next you clarify your purpose or why you are here. You identify and imagine why you are known as an extraordinarily successful sales person in your marketplace and you visualize it.

Your vision of your success with a winning mindset in sales will occur when, given who you are, what is most important to you, and why you are here, you visualize yourself experiencing and achieving successful sales in your marketplace. Then, when you put this winning mindset of sales into action in the present, you will achieve the successful sales results you want. Your clarity of vision will propel your results higher because when you have clarity of vision you have impact. Your vision of your compelling future becomes your catalyst for your sales excitement today! Your vision of your winning mindset of sales becomes your reality!

About Dr. Bill Newman

Dr Bill Newman is president of Executive Beacon, Inc. an executive development company that works with executive teams and their leaders who want to maximize results in growth and performance. Bill is a consulting psychologist, executive coach, and expert in leadership development who speaks professionally. As a consultant, facilitator and speaker, Bill helps CEOs, presidents, and executives inspire and lead to greatness in their corporations. Bill's customized executive development programs, keynote speeches, and business presentations address inspirational leadership, motivational change management, peak performance, the winning mindset in sales, and corporate trust. His programs have been effective for producing sustainable results in growth and performance, and he has been featured in business magazines such as Forbes, Inc. *and* Success; *in major newspapers such as* USA Today, *and* The Wall Street Journal; *on radio programs such as National Public Radio's Morning Edition; and on major television networks such as CBS. Bill is a member of the National Speakers Association and a member of the Board of Directors of the New England Speakers Association*

Contact Information:
Dr. Bill Newman
Executive Beacon, Inc.
5 Market Square, Suite 101
Amesbury, MA 01913
Phone: 1-800-908-2009
Fax: (978) 834-0990
E-mail: Bill@ExecutiveBeacon.com
Website: www.ExecutiveBeacon.com

Selling Tools

by D.J. Harrington, CSP

Many years ago there was a very well-known sales trainer by the name of J. Douglas Edwards. He would tell audiences that his favorite topic to speak on was closing the sale.

He would tell large groups here in the United States and in Europe, "Whoever speaks first after the closing question," then he would pause and the whole audience would yell back at him, "LOSES."

Edwards taught thousands of salespeople around the world a technique that began, "Would you like to use my pen or yours?" He used this technique in order to elicit a minor decision for a major one. He would roll his pen towards the customer, who would make the minor decision of, "would you like to use my pen or yours?" by picking up the pen. Picking up the pen was a sign the customer had bought.

I started my chapter with a memory of J. Douglas Edwards because, if I were asked to write on my favorite topic, it would be my personal journey of selling. I have been asked, and now I write to you on that very topic.

I first started selling while I was in college when I came up with a prescription form that I sent out to every doctor, dentist, and chiropractor in town. The prescription form worked great, and it is what made me different from every other person who was selling at that time. I was working part time for a Chevrolet dealership in Florida. One day, the owner went to his local Kiwanis Club meeting, and one of the chiropractors who had received my prescription, his was for a new Chevrolet Suburban, sat next to him. This was their conversation:

"My office and I thought it was great idea!" said the doctor.

Jerry, the owner, asked, "Who sent it to you?"

"One of your people," replied the doctor.

Jerry demanded again, "Who sent it to you?"

The doctor remembered and answered, "D.J. Harrington was the salesman."

Jerry was furious. He had not given me permission to do anything of the kind. While dessert was being served later, a lady who booked appointments for every doctor at the medical center in town came by to talk to Jerry. She told him that they, too, got a prescription for one of the doctors at the center. She wanted to know if she and her family qualified since she worked at the center.

At this point, Jerry was very upset with me. He got in his beautiful Chevrolet truck and pulled out of the Kiwanis parking lot. He was headed to the dealership to yell at me. Suddenly the city attorney pulled up behind Jerry and blocked him from leaving.

"What can I do for you today?" asked Jerry.

The city attorney replied, "Please tell D.J. that my wife and I will be by tonight about 6:15."

Then Jerry asked, "Did he send you a prescription also?"

"No," replied the attorney, "he sent me a summons."

"A WHAT!!" Jerry gasped.

"Yeah, he asked me to come down to take an affidavit on a new Chevrolet. Jerry, he summoned me to the dealership, and everyone in my office thought it was so clever. I called him that moment and told him I would try for tonight. My wife just called and told me tonight at 6:15 would be great, so I saw you here at Kiwanis and thought I would pass the message on to D.J. through you."

Jerry drove slowly out of the parking lot, thinking about the loose cannon he had working for him, uncertain of what I was going to do next. When Jerry got back to the dealership, he called the sales manager, my so-called buddy, Mark Kowalski, into his office. Jerry asked Mark if he knew what I had done and if he had approved any of it. Mark told Jerry that he was unaware of it and that there were other things I had done, which he was not fully aware of. He told Jerry that I was in class and that I would be working three to eight p.m. that night.

Jerry normally went to play golf at two on Tuesdays, but he was so enraged with me that he cancelled his tee time and waited for me to arrive. The receptionist was told that as soon as I got there, I was to be told to go straight to Jerry's office.

When I arrived, I had to explain the prescription for doctors, the summons for attorneys, and the birthday cards I had been sending out to people who had bought cars two years ago or longer whose salesperson was no longer at the dealership. You see, I sent birthday cards to cars. They read, "Happy Birthday! No — No not you, your car. Wishing you and your car another great year."

The note told previous customers that the salesperson who had helped them with their purchase was no longer at the dealership. I wanted to drop them a note and adopt them since they no longer had a representative at the dealership. I was doing nothing more than Xavier did with the Cabbage Patch Dolls. He sent adoption papers home with every newborn Cabbage Patch Doll.

We need to put the fun back into our selling process. I have to admit, every day I add more tools to my collection. I bought infant sized shoes at Wal-Mart. I would send one to people with a note attached that read, "Now that I have one shoe in the door, let's talk about getting both in." People would call me all the time to tell me how clever that idea was. I also had socks that I'd mail out with a printed message on them that read, "We Will Knock Your Socks Off."

I was speaking in Minneapolis, Minnesota, for Damon Motor Homes. A young man five or six rows from the front said, "That's what you did in college. What have you done lately?" The people at Damon were furious with him and his sales manager reprimanded him, but I told him it wasn't a problem. I have a very serious outlook on life. We must always keep learning. I use an expression in my classes that goes like this: "The difference between a rut and a grave is the depth. Some of us are in the grave and don't even know it." Then I looked at the young man and told him that I was going to tell him what I did last month to sell a Damon Motor Coach.

I was eating dinner with the sales manager of a good-sized recreational vehicle location. One of the newer salesmen came over to the table and the sales manager asked, "What happened to the family you were showing that kitchen slide-out to?" The salesman answered, "They wanted to go home and sleep on it." I waited for the sales manager to speak up, but nothing came out of his mouth. I thought he would give the salesperson a tip to help him overcome an adversity like that. About thirty minutes went by, and an older man who had been in sales a long time gave the sales manager a similar answer to the same question.

Let me ask you, has anyone ever said those words to you? The sales manager never gave any suggestions on dealing with this response from a customer. A few weeks later, Damon Motor Homes management asked me to go back out to that same location to train. First, I went online and ordered discounted pillow cases and had 12 dozen printed with these messages:

"Check up from the Neck-Up"

"We sell Fun"

"Attitude is everything"

"Sleep on it"

The people at the dealership went crazy over them. Yes, I gave away pillowcases at my seminar. The new salesperson I had first encountered loved the tip and asked for a pillowcase to take home. So I gave him one and signed it "God Bless, D.J. Harrington." Every day these kinds of things happen to you when you are in the "Real World of Selling."

I have an 8"x11" oversized "while you were out" message pad. If someone doesn't return my call within two to three days after I have called multiple times, I will send the person one of my famous message pad sheets. At the bottom in the remarks section I write, "I spoke to God this morning; why can't I talk to you?" You would be amazed; within minutes many people call me back laughing, wanting to get the message pads. They in turn can send them out to people who don't return their phone calls.

I was speaking at a convention in Salt Lake City, Utah, and mentioned what I write at the bottom of my fax sheet, "I spoke to God this morning; why can't I talk to you?" A gentleman in the back of the class yelled, "Here in Salt Lake that would be a local call." The entire audience laughed. I caught on about thirty minutes later.

St. Petersburg, Florida

I wanted so much to be selected to be the trainer of a very large group of stores in St. Petersburg, Florida. I first gave them a prescription to cure their lack of sales. My prescription would be to hire me. Next, I sent a shoe followed by a large fax sheet when I didn't get any returned calls. I knew they were still looking for a phone trainer and I knew I fit the bill. I called the director of Human Resources and was told in a very blunt, matter-of-fact way, "Listen, Harrington, we all loved your shoe in the door. We thought your prescription and fax was clever; all that stuff was great. But here is what we do. We take all of the applicants' names and put them in a big pot. We stir it a few times, and if your name comes out we call you for the next interview."

Back in Atlanta, my daughter Erin, who was too young to drive at the time, needed to go to Pier One to get a gift for one of her teachers. As Erin was going through the store, I went over to the discount table. There in the middle of the marked down goods were two big wooden spoons. It looked like a small dog had nibbled on the end of one of the spoons. I bought both spoons, sanded down the ends, and stained them to look like new. Putting them in a large flower box, I mailed them to Florida with a note that read, "The next time you are stirring the pot, please use my spoons and think of me."

It went over great. All the managers who saw the spoons at their monthly meeting said, "We need to hire this guy. He is making us think outside the box."

I would like to add something right about now. A lot of speakers tell you to think outside the box. Some tell you not just to think outside the box, but also to do outside the box. I have found that some people don't even know where the box is, and when they find it, they trip over it.

I spent over five years training at that company in Florida, and I am very proud of my work and the people I helped grow.

When I am asked if I ever think I go a little overboard, my answer is, "Not just once but a few times." For example, one day I had an appointment with Walter McDaniel at Uniroyal Tire in Detroit. Mr. McDaniel was looking for a speaker for an upcoming convention. I told his secretary to put my name on the list of interested speakers. After all, I had worked in the sales force at Uniroyal before; in fact I had won number one salesperson of the year and had broken all new distribution records. Who better to speak than someone who used to work for Uniroyal? Mr. McDaniel was nice enough to meet with me. I set my appointment for July 22 at 1:15 p.m. at the Jefferson Avenue office in Detroit.

I had spoken the night before in Toledo, Ohio. So I got up early the next morning, drove to Detroit, got a hotel room, shaved, showered, put on a nice suit and was in Mr. McDaniel's office on

Vince Lombardi time. (Ten minutes early!) I had called the day before to confirm my appointment, so you can imagine my surprise when by 2:30 there was still no word from Mr. McDaniel. Not even a phone call to say he had gotten delayed somewhere. Finally at three I took off, madder than blazes. How dare he stand up the former number one salesperson!

I could not just drive back south. I had already rented a room for the night so I decided to go back to the hotel, where I had a pity party for myself. I felt miserable. Then I thought, "What are you doing? Are you going to let this little setback get the best of you?" I took off my suit and went back to Jefferson Avenue to get a good look at the brick they used to build the building. I drove to a materials warehouse, where I purchased a brick in the same color. Borrowing a hammer, I proceeded to smash the brick to pieces; I put the pieces in a bag, drove to FedEx, and then sent the bag to Mr. McDaniel with a note.

The following day I called his office to see if the package had arrived.

"Oh it got here all right," commented the secretary. "In fact it got here before I did and Mr. McDaniel himself signed for it."

I proceeded to tell her, "This is a weather call, whether I should show up for my appointment or not."

Then she asked, "D.J., did you forget Mr. McDaniel has a glass top on his desk?"

"Oh my goodness," I gasped, "did it break?"

"No, no, he opened the package and all the little pieces fell out. One by one the little bricks ricocheted off the glass and onto the floor. It looked like a bomb went off in his office. Your note was the last thing to fall out of the box, and it landed smack dab in the middle of his desk," She chuckled.

My note read that I was outside on Jefferson Avenue, hitting my head against the wall, waiting for my 1:15 appointment, and then asked when I could come up and see him.

I want all of you reading this chapter to understand, I believe you should lead by example and judge by results. I tell sales classes every day, when I hear excuses from them on why they didn't make the sale or close the deal, "I don't want to hear about the birthing pains, I just want to see the baby."

Being from Atlanta, the home of America's team, The Atlanta Braves, we can buy a tomahawk or hatchet on any street corner. I have sent a hatchet in a box with a note that says, "Let's bury the hatchet and start working together." Selling is a science; we can always work at being better salespeople. Find your niche, and promote it for all it's worth.

Before giving a presentation in Canada to Toyota, I heard two trainers speaking. They had asked what size bandage they were going to use to cover the lack of sales that year. I went the concierge of my hotel that night, and he himself drove me to an all-night drug store, where I purchased four different sizes of bandages for my presentation the next day. The presentation was to a panel of ten people who were going to decide who would be the trainer at the next year's conference. When I ended my presentation, I handed out one of the four different sizes of band-aids to each of them and asked, "What size bandages are we going to use, or are we going to correct the problem right now." I got hired.

Ray Pellitier, a Certified Speaking Professional, has taught me how he uses rubber bands. He passes out the rubber bands and blows a whistle. He asks everyone to break the rubber band at the sound of the whistle. Everyone in the room breaks the rubber band. He passes out new rubber bands to everyone. He then asks the people to write their name on the rubber band, their company name, the name of their children, and some way to identify the rubber band as theirs. He then collects them and picks the two strongest people out of the room. He gathers all the rubber bands together and asks the two strong people to break them. It's impossible. Ray tells the whole audience that, individually we can be broken, but together as a team, association, company or church we cannot break. Ray wrote a great book, *Permission to Win*, which features many useful practices. If you can't find the book, call me or send me an e-mail and I'll get you one.

I have put air fresheners in envelopes and told people, "When you want a fresh clean scent of sales, call me." I have sent ringing telephones and asked how much it costs your phone to ring and not have trained people answering it. I have a ton of tips on generating sales. I am proud to be a professional speaker and proud to be American and exuberant to be a salesperson. I can't recall where I first heard this statement, but it still holds true: "Success has u in the middle, and none of what I shared will work unless u do."

About
D.J. Harrington, CSP

D.J. *Harrington, CSP is President of Phone Logic, Inc., an international telemarketing and training company based in Atlanta, GA. He serves as a consultant to over 600 businesses throughout the U.S. D.J. appears every week on ASTN, the national cable training network. Programs focus on prospecting to in-coming calls. As a syndicated columnist for 33 newspapers and* Power Source *magazine, D.J. writes monthly articles that appear from Atlanta to Los Angeles. He is known as Mr. Motivator at General Motors, and by many of his clients as the Gallagher of the speaking circuit. His years as sales trainer and motivator for a variety of companies have provided D.J. with a diverse background which he combines with energy and his dynamic personality to provide memorable presentations for companies such as UniRoyal, General Motors, American Bank Systems, Bloomingdale's, IBM, American Express, Mohawk Carpet, Damon Motor Homes, Auto Services, Inc. and The Original On-Hold Company. D.J. is a member of the National Speakers Association and has earned their Certified Speaking Professional designation.*

Contact Information:
D.J. Harrington, CSP
Phone Logic, Inc.
Phone: (800) 352-5252
Website: www.DJHarrington.com

Resource Listing

Andre L. Beaudoin
Andre Inspires
38 Country Lane
Meriden CT 06451-2711
Phone: (800) 205-6958
Fax: 800-856-4250
E-mail: andre@andreinspires.com
Website: www.andreinspires.com

Mary E. Cremeans, M.B.A.
A&P Group
15580 Oakcrest Circle
Brooksville, FL 34604-8238
Phone: (352) 796-6880
E-mail: shopkeep@quixnet.net

D.J. Harrington, CSP
Phone Logic, Inc.
Phone: (800) 352-5252
Website: www.DJHarrington.com

Dr. Bill Newman
Executive Beacon, Inc.
5 Market Square, Suite 101
Amesbury, MA 01913
Phone: 1-800-908-2009
Fax: (978) 834-0990
E-mail: Bill@ExecutiveBeacon.com
Website: www.ExecutiveBeacon.com

Sara Owens
Promo Pros, Inc.
St. Louis, MO
Phone: (314) 322-6645
Fax: (314) 989-1565
E-mail: sara@promo-pros.com
Website: www.promo-pros.com

Edie Raether, M.S., CSP
Performance PLUS
4717 Ridge Water Court
Holly Springs, NC 27540
Phone: (919) 557-7900
Fax: (919) 557-7999
E-mail: edie@raether.com
Website: www.raether.com

Debra J. Schmidt, M.S.
Spectrum Consulting Group Inc.
P.O. Box 170954
Milwaukee, WI 53217-8086
Phone: (414) 964-3872
Fax: (414) 967-0875
E-mail: deb@theloyaltybuilder.com
Website: www.SpectrumResults.com

Larry Sheldon
Shelco Creative Consulting
951 Glenwood Avenue, Suite 2907
Atlanta, GA 30316-1893
Phone: (404) 624-1721
Fax: (404) 624-1721
E-mail: larrysheldon@shelco.net
Website: www.shelco.net

Albert R. Tetrault, M.B.A.
Chairman, Innovative Strategies Group
P.O. Box 76551
Atlanta, GA 30358
Phone: (770) 310-3175
Fax: (877) 471-1387
E-mail: tetrault@revenue-growth.com
Website: www.revenue-growth.com

Patti Wood, M.A., CSP
2312 Hunting Valley Drive
Decatur, GA 30033
Phone: (404) 371-8228
E-mail: Pattiwood@PattiWood.com
Website: www.PattiWood.com
        www.TheBodyLanguageLady.com

"Everyone lives by selling something."
— Robert Louis Stevenson

"Sell to their needs, not yours."
— *Earl G. Graves*

> "Nothing is impossible."
> — Christopher Reeve

> "Be different, stand out, and work your butt off."
> — Reba McEntire

> "I am the world's worst salesman, therefore, I must make it easy for people to buy."
> —F. W. Woolworth

"The surest foundation of a manufacturing concern is quality. After that, and a long way after, comes cost."
— Andrew Carnegie

"Man does not only sell commodities, he sells himself."
— Erich Fromm

"Business has only two functions — marketing and innovation."
— Peter Drucker

"If you find it in your heart to care for someone else, you have succeeded."
— Maya Angelou

"Ask for what you want and be prepared to get it."
— Maya Angelou

"The secret to closing huge sales is found in one tiny word: ask"
—Doug Smart